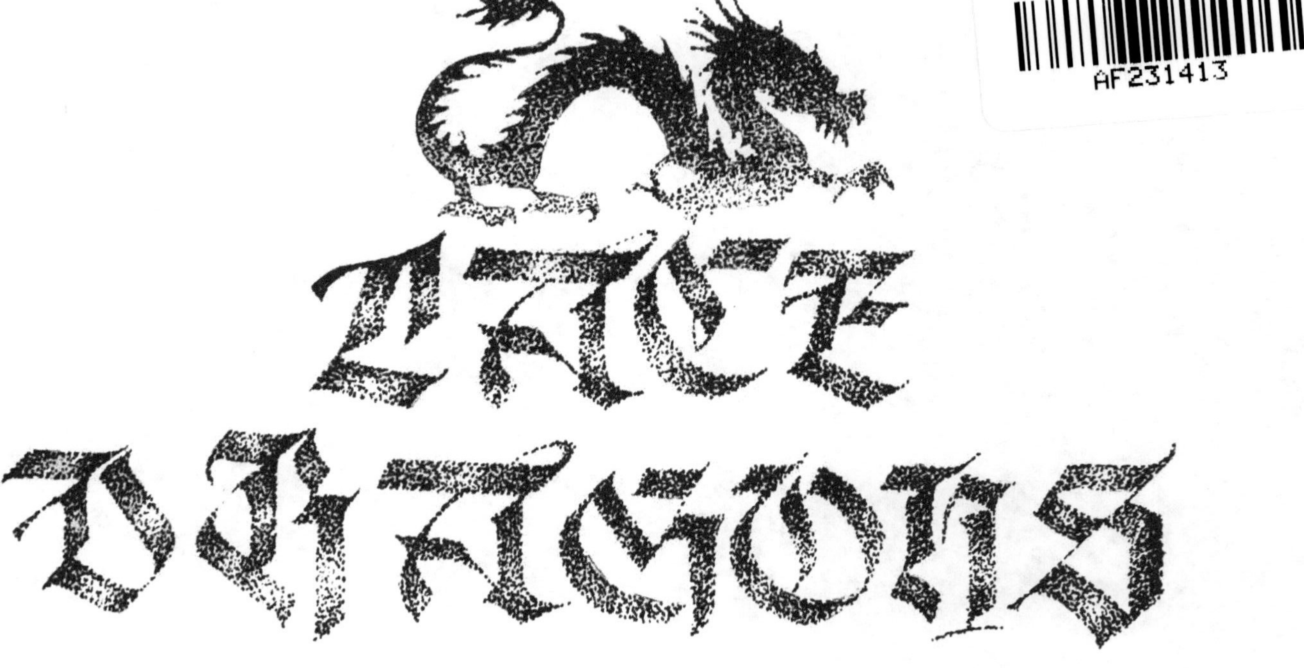

POEMS & PRISON ART

LILY J. NOONAN & GREGG STONE, EDITORS

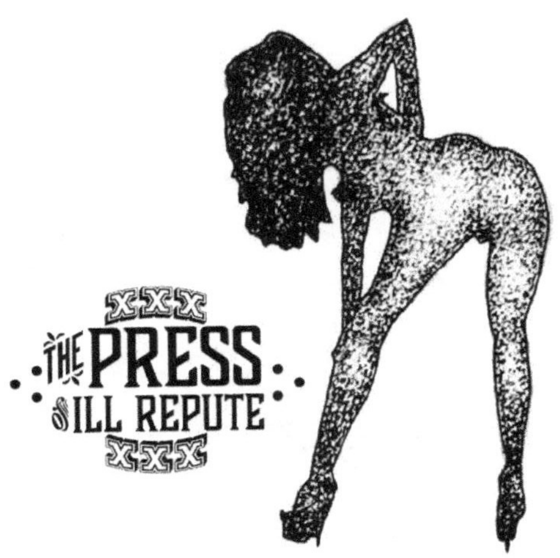
XXX
THE PRESS
OF ILL REPUTE
XXX

This book is dedicated to all the souls who graciously

offer their delights to anyone who can pay the price.

Most of the poems in this collection were written by Rachel Wrong, an American woman who worked as a prostitute in Tijuana, Mexico. There are other poems within this collection written by one of her clients.

The illustrations are by inmates within the California penal system.

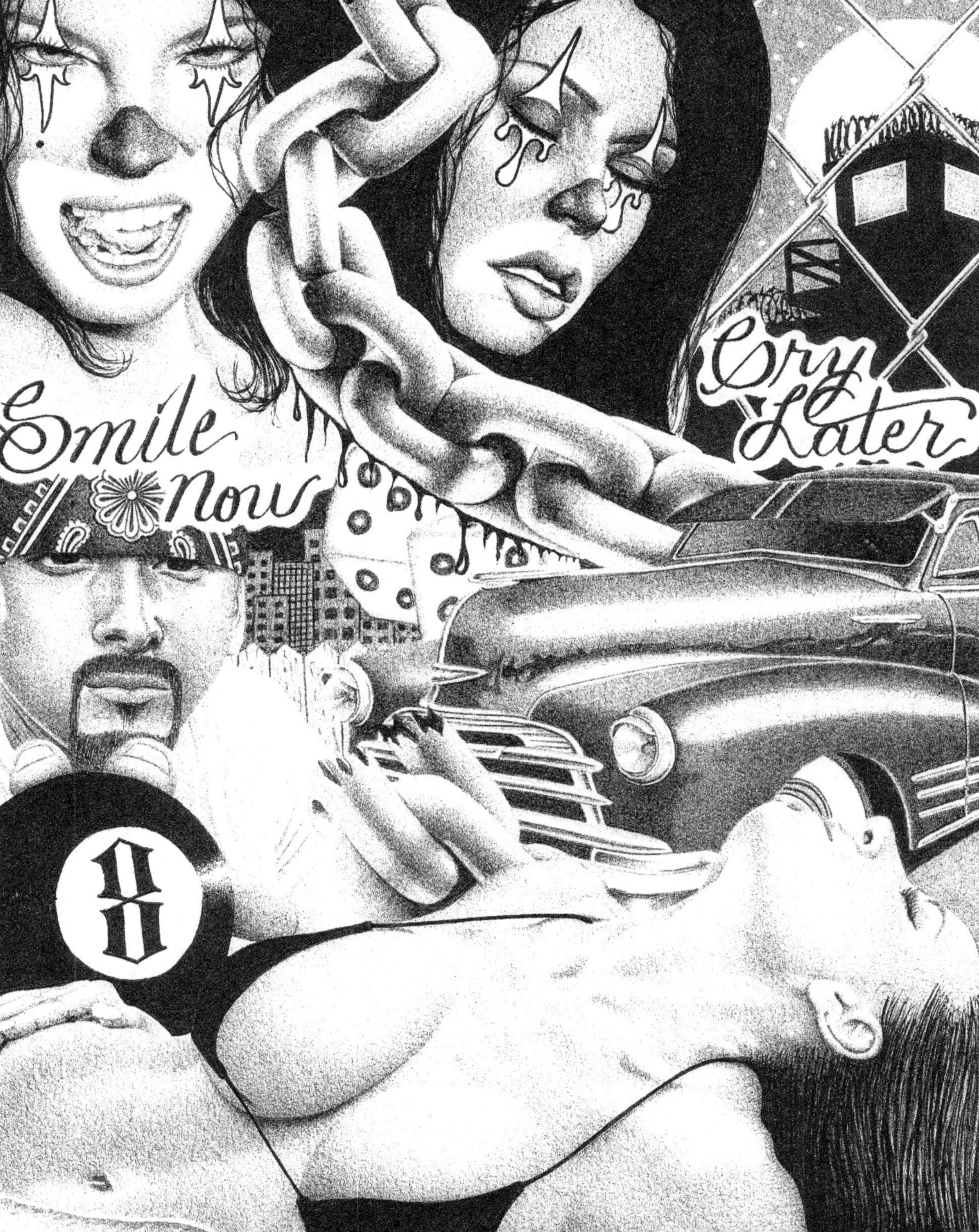

Smile Now
Cry Later

A past doomed to be repeated

Breathless and defeated

Oh, this space is taken,

but somewhere over there, you can be seated

Just happy to not have been told "beat it!"

from the dope dealer's house where I frequent.

I got a monster following me

And now I know why they told me not to feed it

I'd like to have friends and they're so costly

But I've paid the price so now come with me, friend,

and no complaints about me being bossy

Many times accused falsely

Back me in a corner and I can get quite ballsy

Chasing lies

Don't believe in goodbyes

Follow me to the bedroom and I'll get you to not be so shy

Pick and pry

Choose a side

Living to die

Hiding to cry

Too many questions without answers so I'll never know why

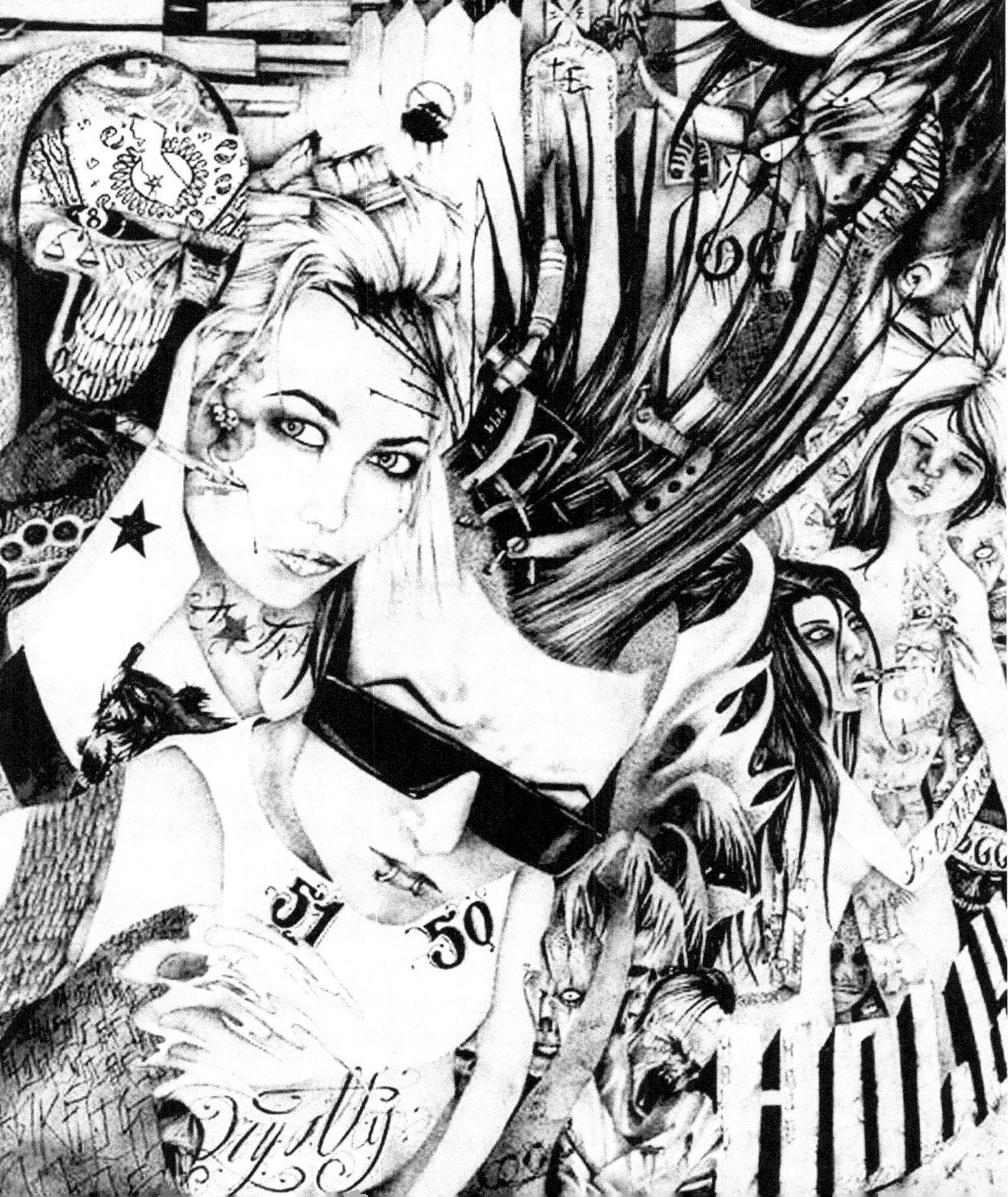

RUBIK'S CUBE

This ship is sinking and we all are going to drown!

Down

Down

Down

Down into a bottomless hole

Overtaken by fears

Hold back the tears

This hole is as dark and empty as my damaged soul

Any pain you've ever felt before won't compare

This sadness is tenfold

Shivering cold

Dirty

Thirsty

Jerking

but all I want is a full syringe

Life without drugs is a Rubik's cube

A game for one

And a game I can't win

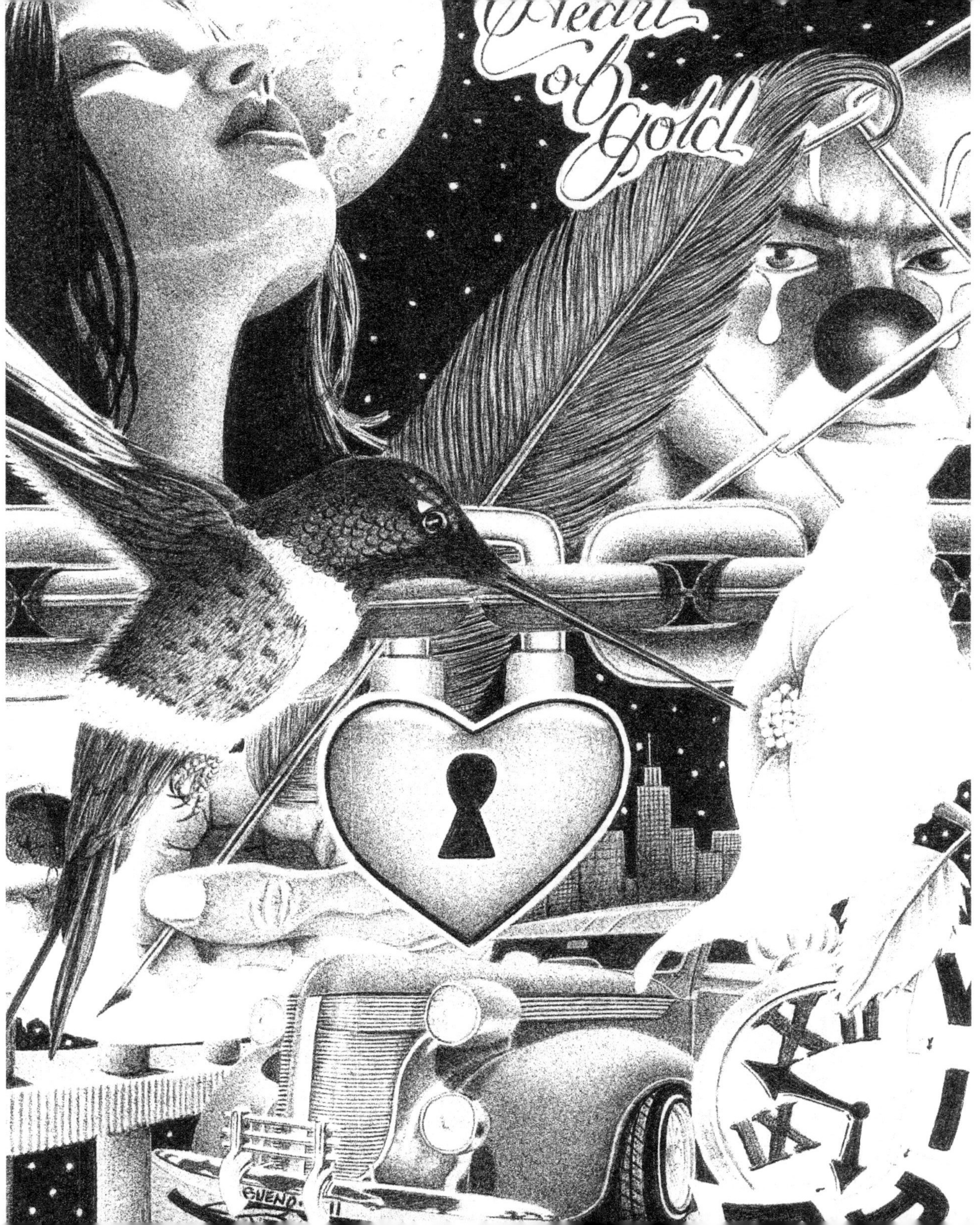

Heart
of
Gold
BUENO

Never enough

Always too much

Don't want to be bothered with that stuff

just because I'm empty inside

No longer who I once was

Push and shove

Pull the plug

Wicked is as wicked does

Drips of blood

Did I fail to entertain?

I knew I was a dud

A stick in the mud

Robbed of love

Wakened by a gentle nudge

"Hello, it's Drugs, and I'm your best bud."

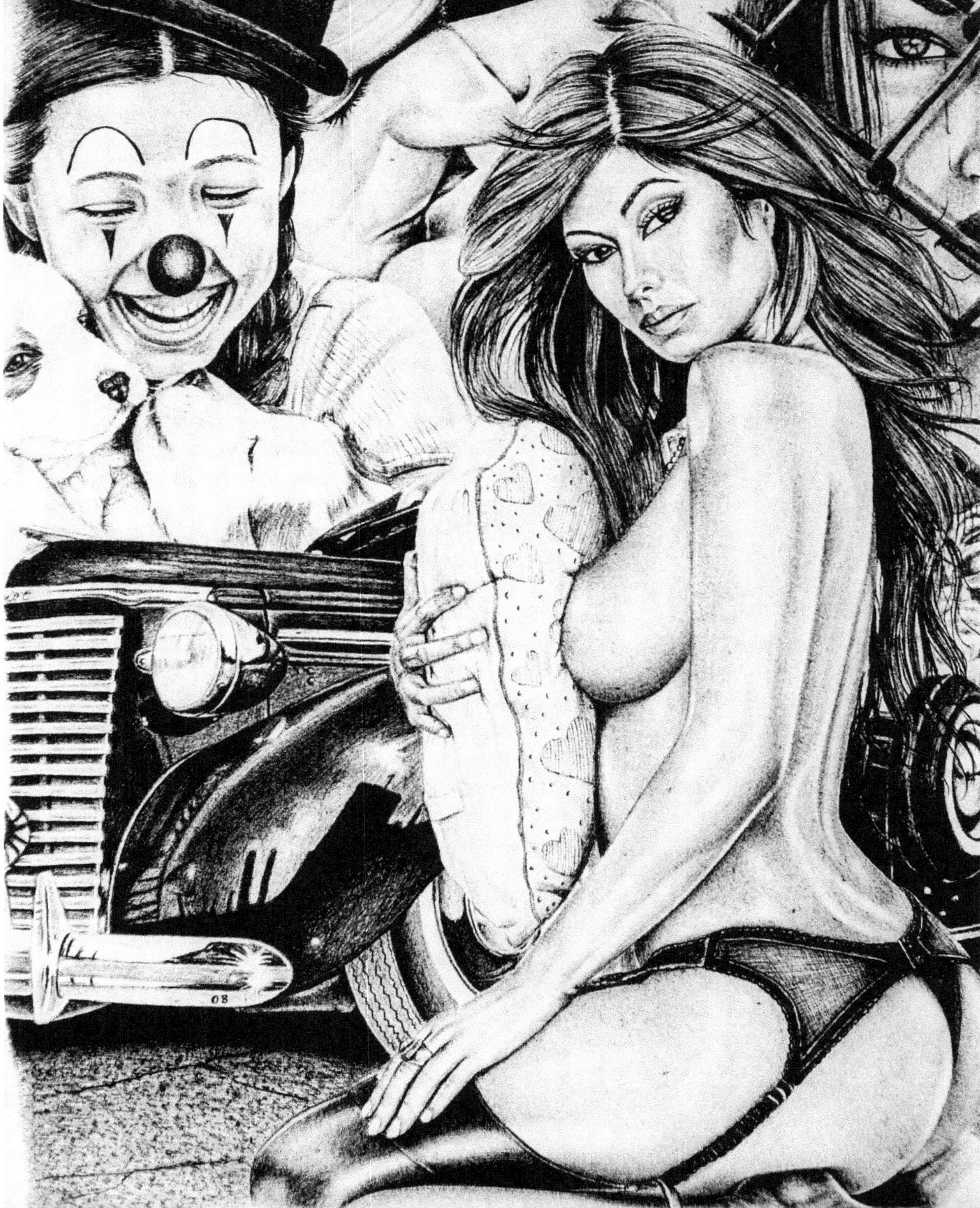

TRUTH

A pile of cash
could make my happiness last
Money, oh so lovely!
Always just out of grasp
Running through my fingers
way too fast

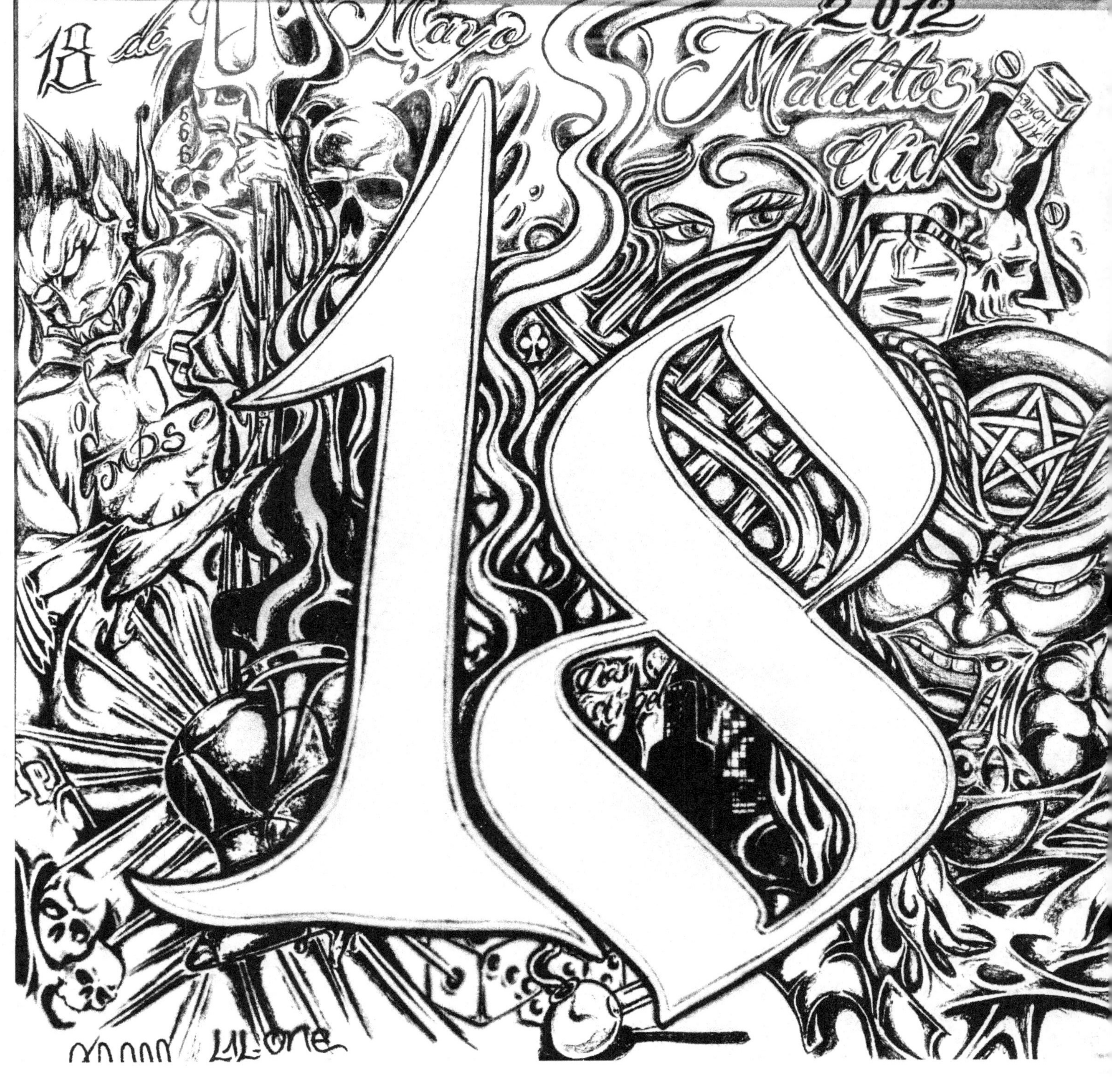
18 de Mayo
2012
Malditos Click
LIL-One

It is the end
but who gives a fuck
when you're surrounded by meaningless friends?
Came to win
But now I'm dying in sin
You can always count on me to forgive a big pig
and to keep my eyes blind to what you did
This is how I live
Been acquainted with pain since I was a kid
Been around the block more than once
I'm not fucked by your fibs
It could all end here and now with just a simple "I did"
Stable as the wind
You've taken all I have to give

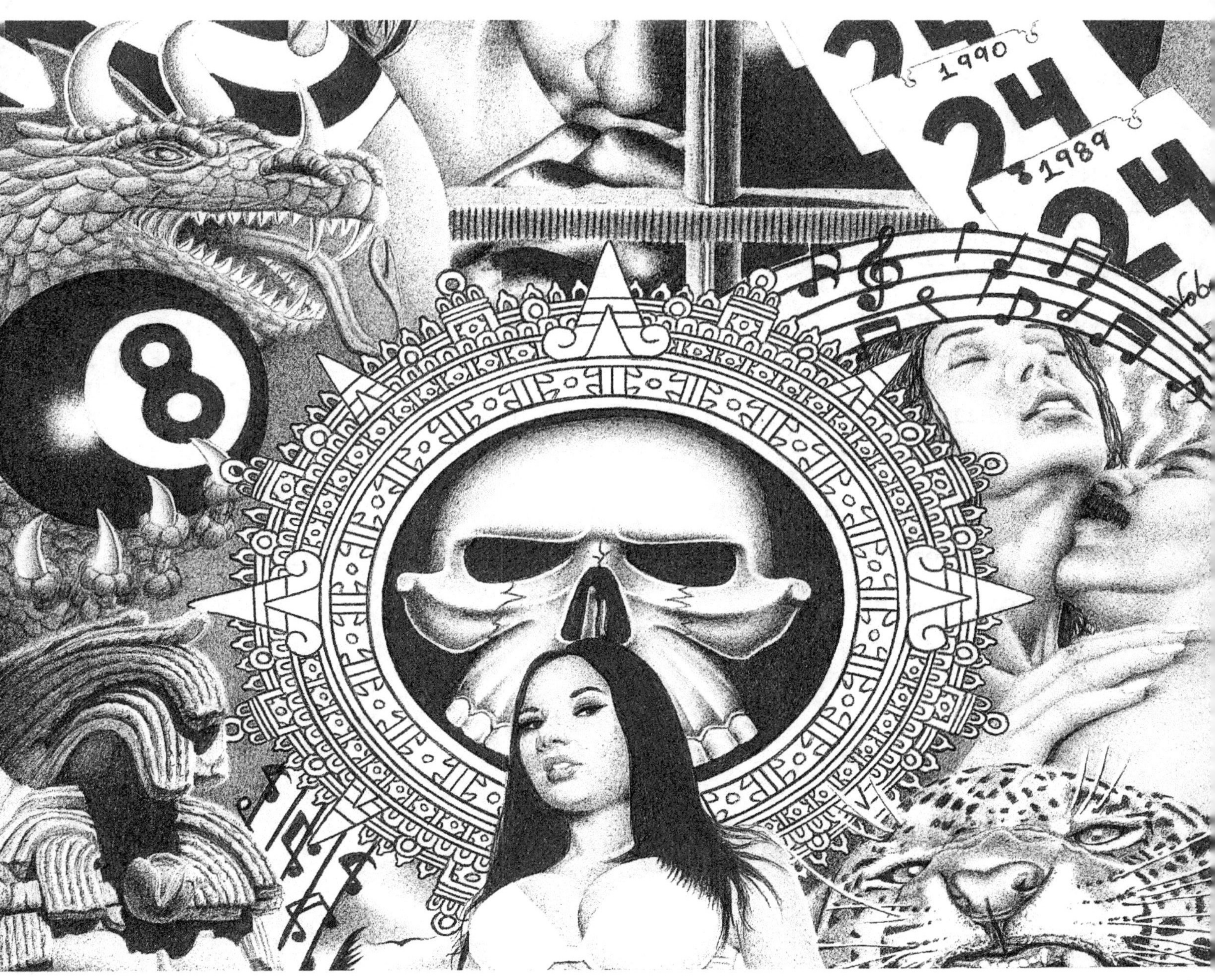
1990
1989
8

TIME

Easy come

Easy go

Plant my seeds and watch them grow

Oh, the things I'd change if only I had known

Flesh and bone

Sticks and stones

Neglect and darkness destroyed my garden

Leaving me alone

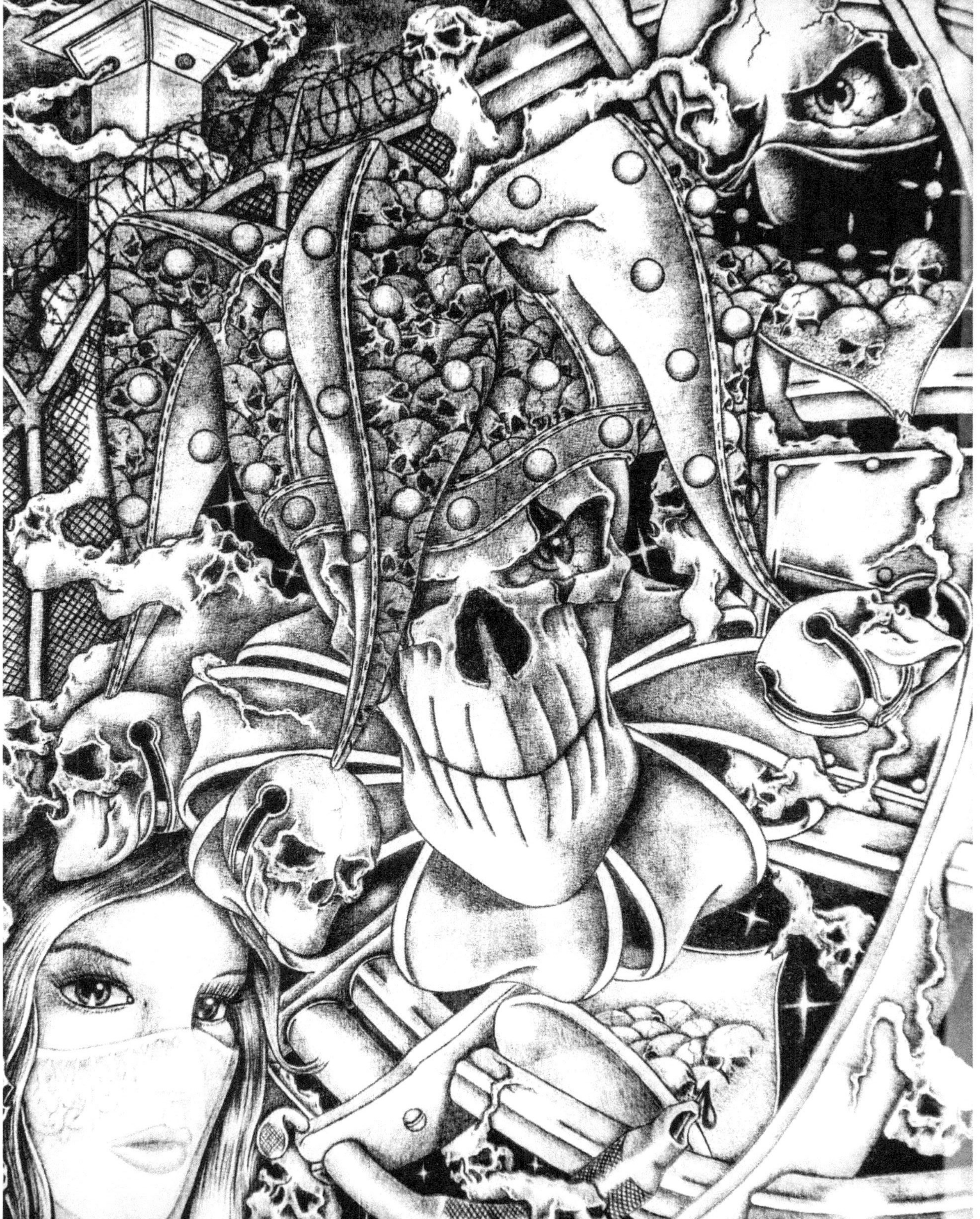

JUSTICE FOR NONE

Running faster and faster in a race never won
Spin the barrel, point the gun
When is enough?
When can you walk away and finally be done?
Victorious in battle, but the war rages on
Careful when you touch me
You could break our carefully crafted bond
My intentions are pure
but I'm sure
there is one among us who is nothing but a con
So sing your song and prove me wrong
It's almost time for me to get on along
and I'm most positive
you'll all be much more comfortable
with your plastic smiles, lies, and crooked ties
once I'm gone

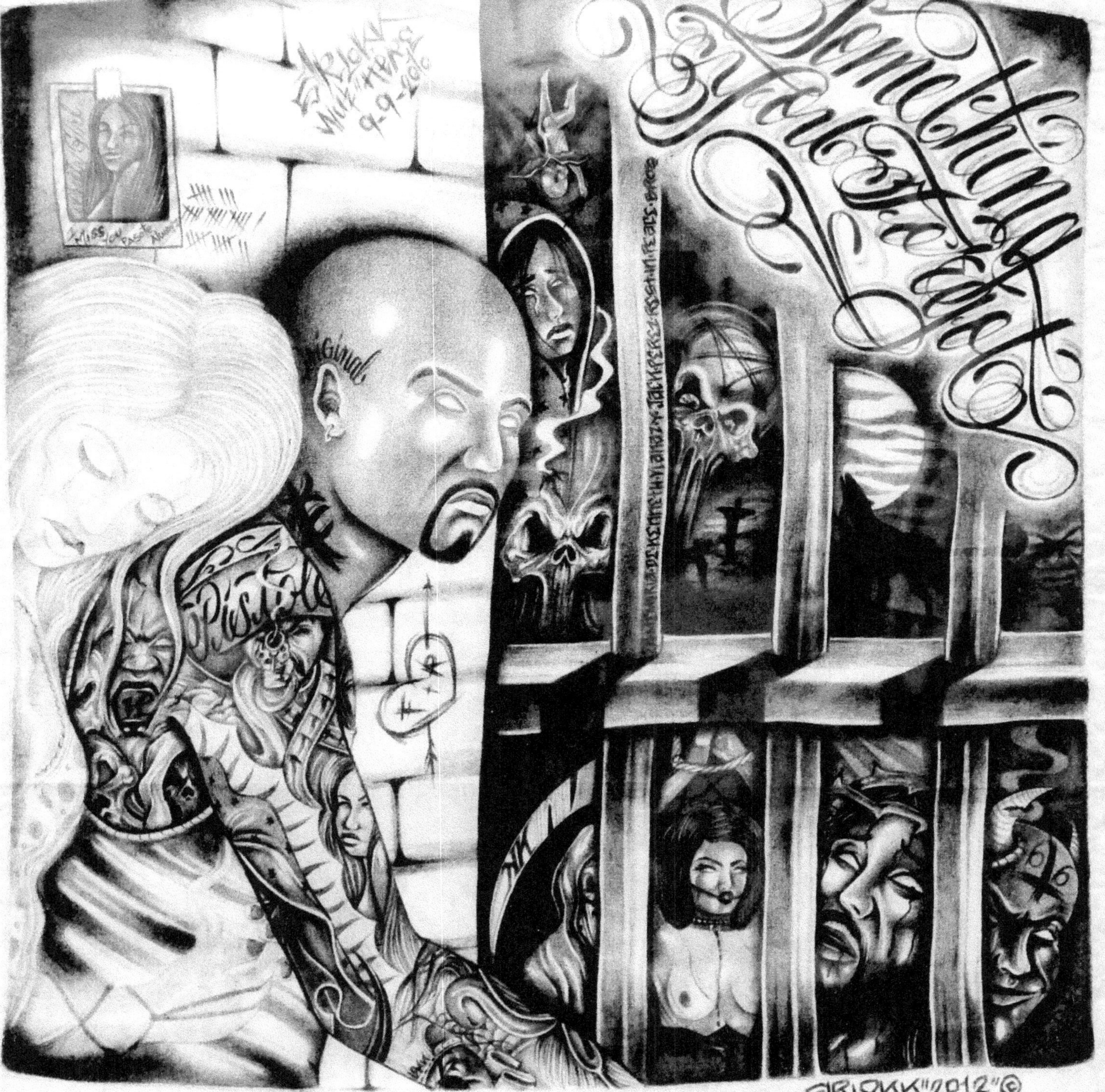
Sixlokk
Muk"Mens"
9-9-2010
Original
SIRLOKK "2012" ©

SO FUCKING TIRED

A soul of ashes from a burnt-out fire
This situation has grown dire
Broken brain needs to be rewired
Clocks ticking on an eternal timer
Branded a worthless liar
Selling neatly wrapped bullshit and there's a ton of buyers
You ignited sparks inside of me
You removed a blindfold from my face
so I could see a Love so wonderful
it must be a dream
Then you withdrew your Love
and now I'm in need

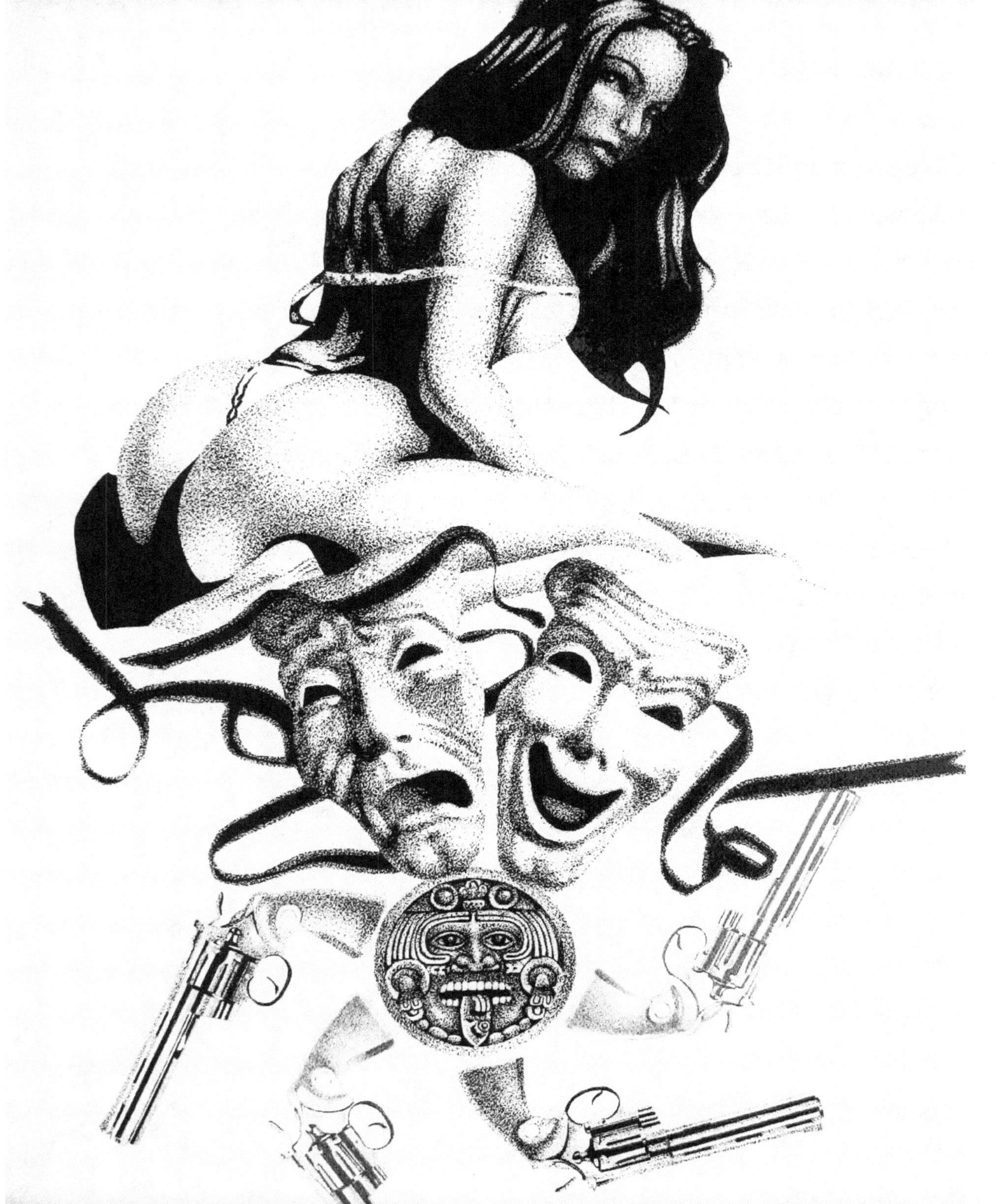

LOVE TIMES TWO

Love me slowly
Love me boldly
Love me with a heart fully showing
Love me in a world so coldly
My body's clay, and I love the way you mold me
Love me with the deepest passion
Love me with a love that's lasting
Love me in a world so enchanting
Love me in the play you're casting
Love me falling or love me dancing
We'll feast on love when we're fasting

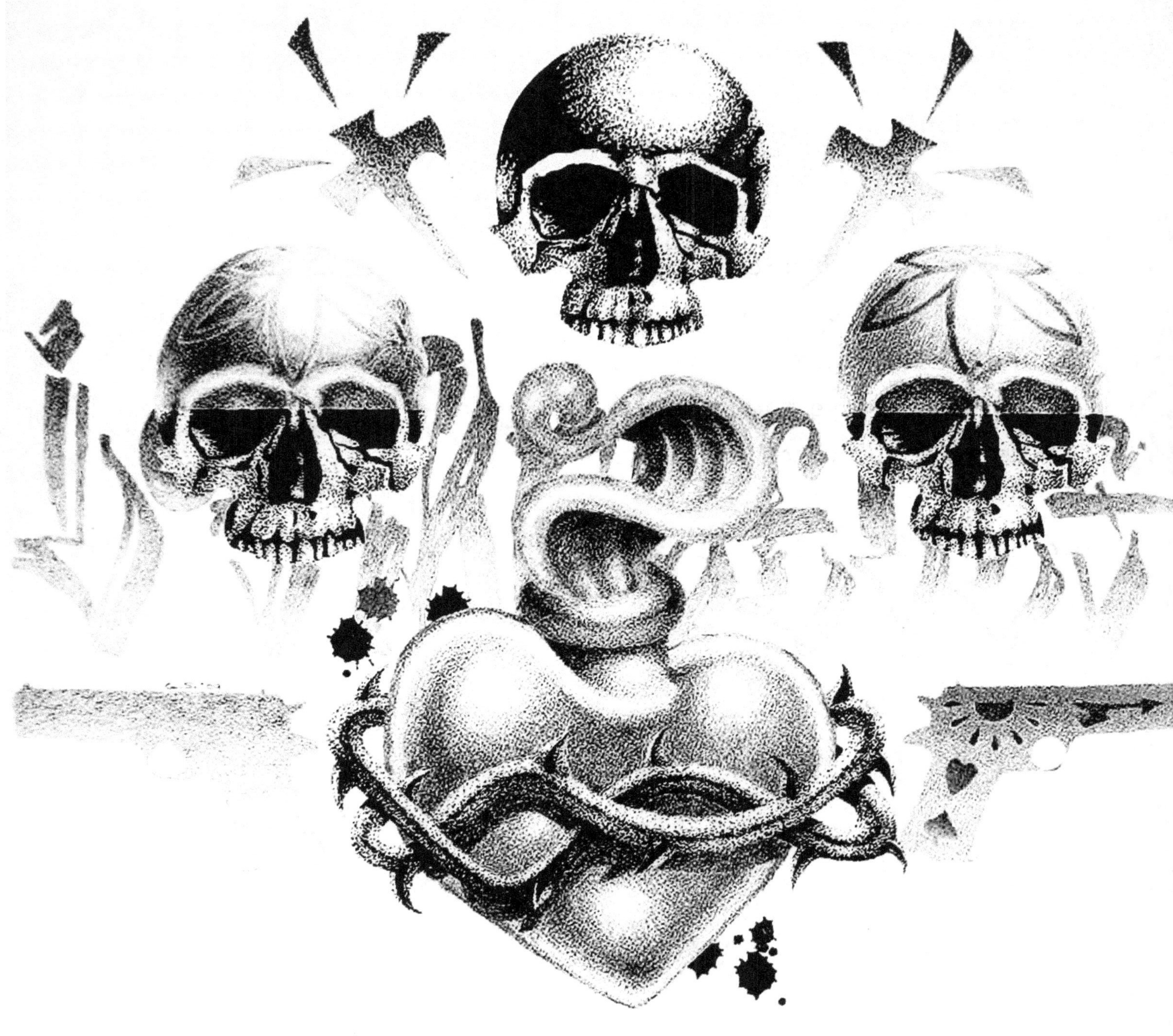

REPLY TO LOVE TIMES TWO

Nix, upon this romantic mix
I'd rather see you sucking dicks
That corny slop is a flop and smells worse than a dirty cock
Love me through your menstrual flowing
Love me when the cows are lowing
Love me this
Love me that
Love gives me a heart attack
Love me when I only got ten bucks, you fucking rat
Love me thin, love me fat, tit for tat, you little brat
Love me with all your feeling
If I cum too hard, we'll pull your head out of the ceiling
Love me like I wanna feel
Tickle my balls and make me squeal
Love is all I'm living for: a dirty room and greasy whore
There is one love beyond compare
That's when a "Trick" is finished and pays her fare

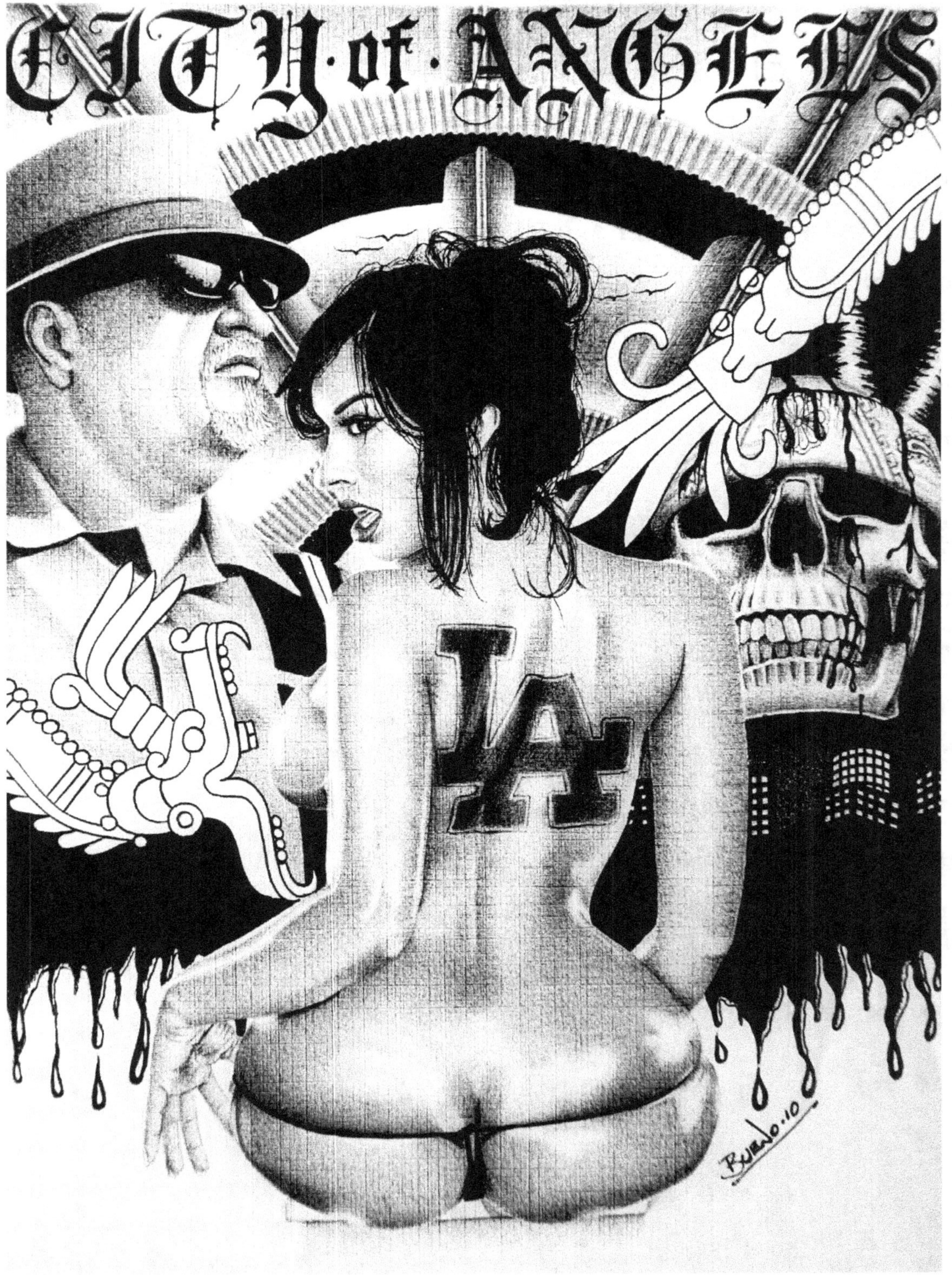

CITY of ANGELS

Blisters on my nimble fingers
A lovely storybook dreamer
Chipping away layers of pain
Profit and loss
Solitary and fame
Tallying up my losses
But there's nothing there to add for my gain

Choose your player carefully before you're thrown into the game
And while we're on the subject
I'm extremely dissatisfied with the player I've been playing
With whom may I make a complaint?
My player's weak
A prisoner with unbreakable chains
and you're telling me I'm stuck with this person I can't change?
Well, I've still got my turn
Though long ago my luck spiraled down the drain
Yes, all I do is mostly complain

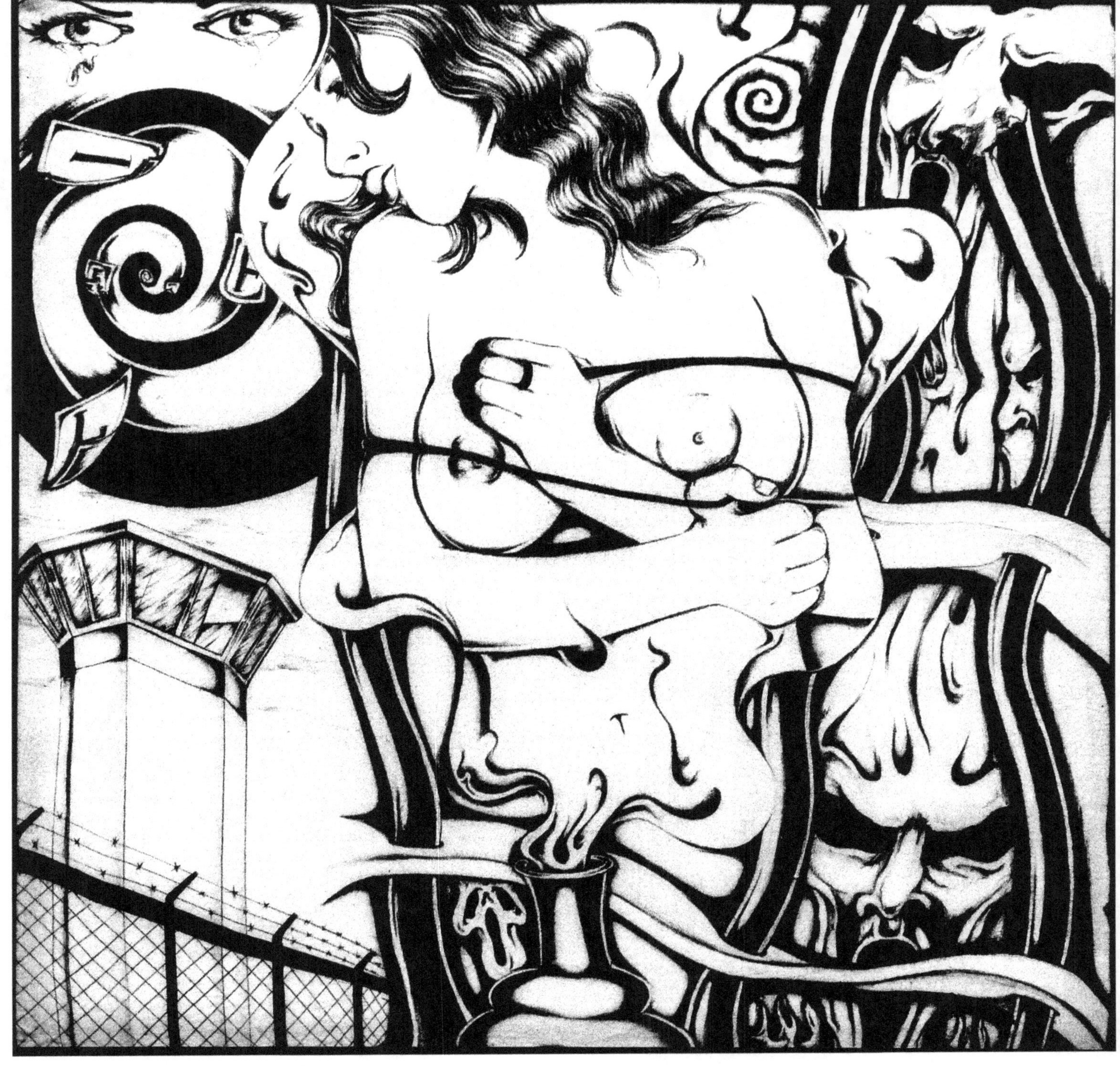

Drowning in my own filthy misery

I'm here to ruin everyone's day

I won't be satisfied until you all feel just as shitty

Now don't insult me with your petty pity

Quitters deserve no pitying

and I'm the biggest quitter of all those quitting

Matter o' fact, I even quit the quitting

I'll die a miserable lonely death well before fifty

says that small voice dwelling deep inside me where it's

frightening, dark, and dingy

Isn't intuition nifty?

I have a knack for doing those things that are silently killing

You'll never leave scot-free

because everyone will receive statements for services rendered

when I begin my billing

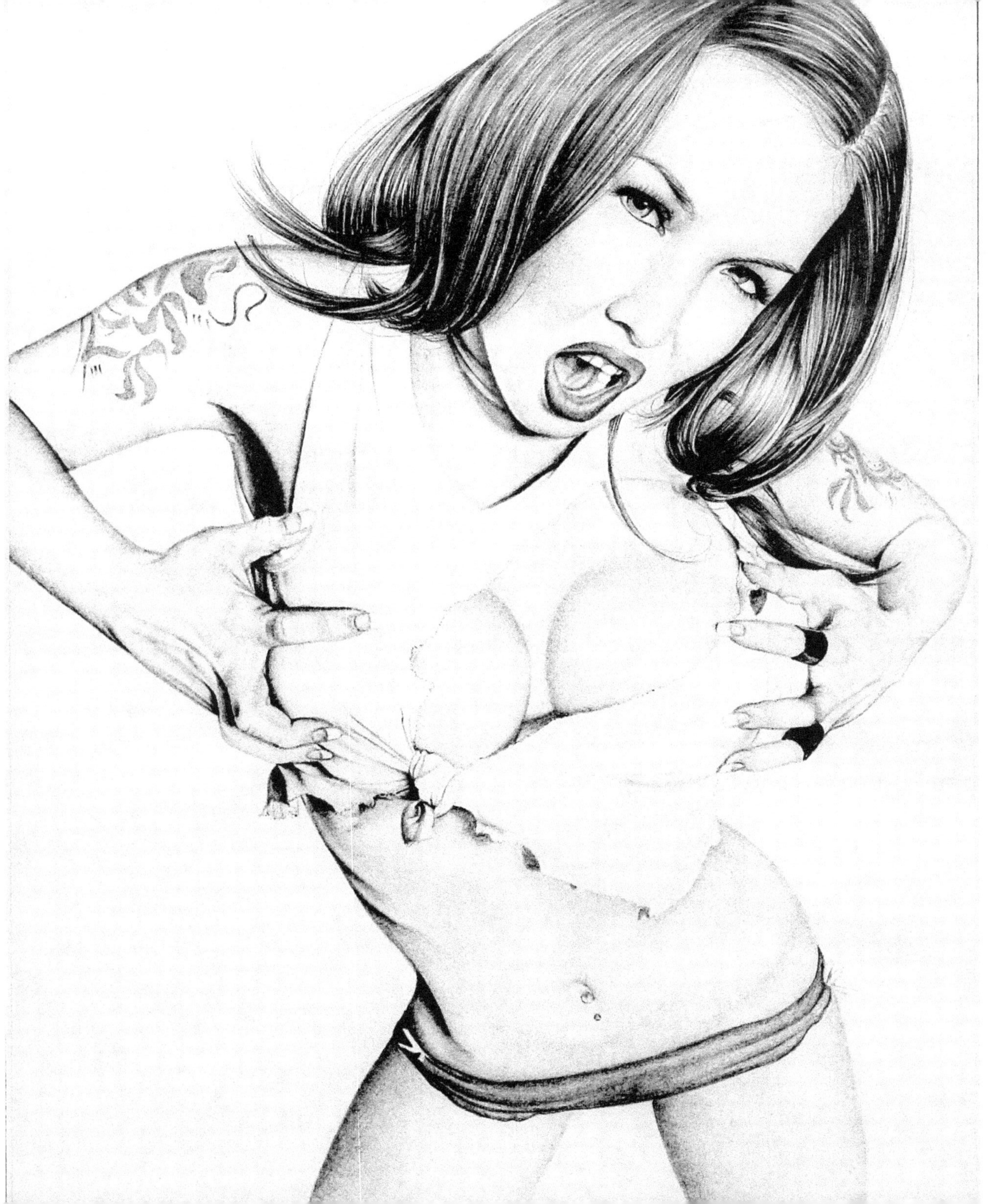

No such thing as one of a kind
Stored so many dreams for another time
Can I hit Rewind?
Shall I knock again at your door?
Passion and love my only crime
Many years have passed by without a sign
of my inner life's shine
Feeling like a total bore
and no, I don't need your pity
Another day gone shitty
though I used to be so smart, beautiful, and witty

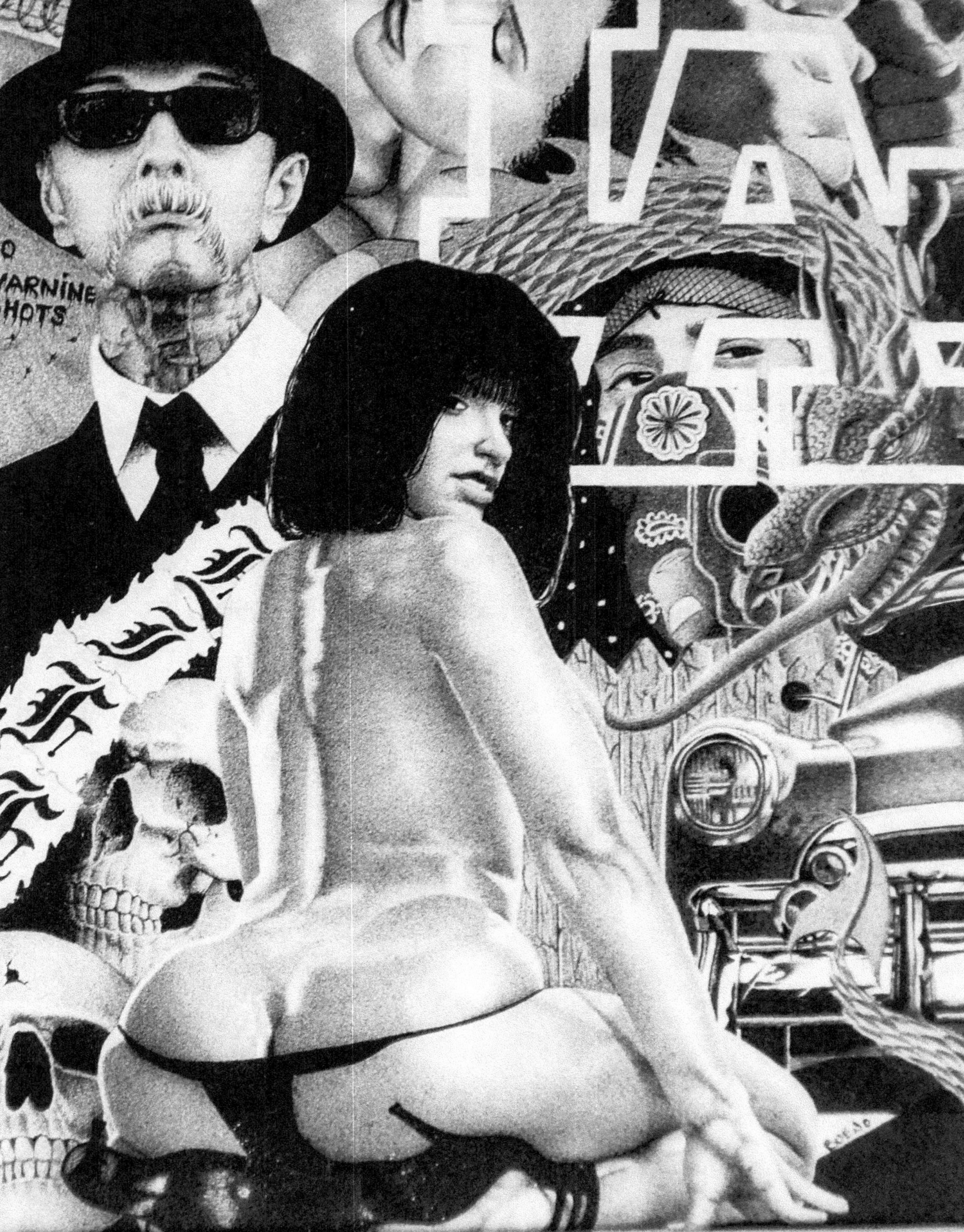
NO
WARNING
SHOTS

Mostly alone

Unaware of the time

Always getting high

Sadness creeps around my chest

Repressed tears for all that's been lost

Releasing years of life that's already passed me by

For that, I cry

I cry

I cry

I get high

and then, I cry

Why am I such a fuck-up?

Why?

Why?

I've been calling out to this God for years

But the only thing I hear is the shaky hurting voice of mine

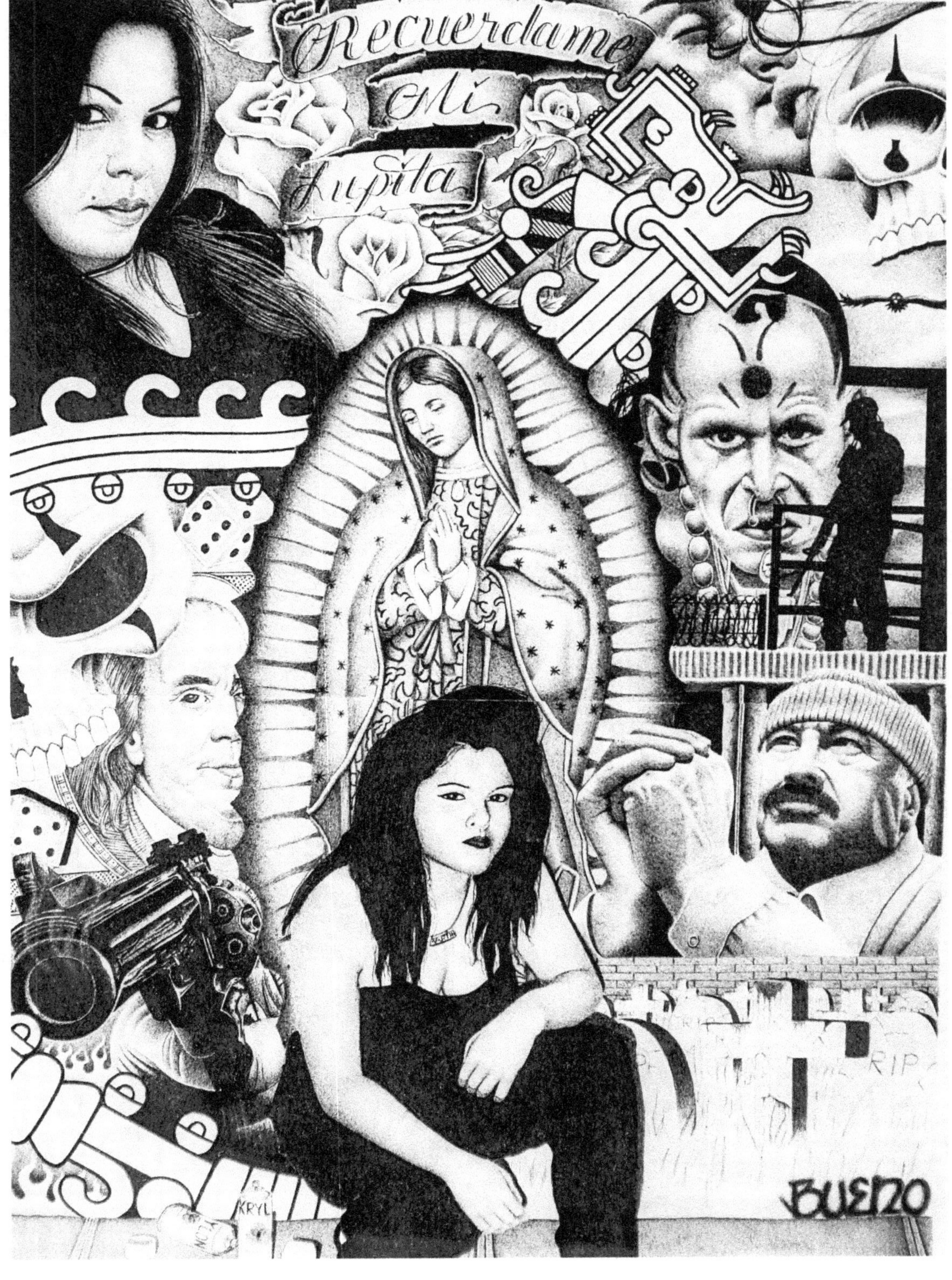

Recuerdame
Mi
Lupita
BUENO

Trapped inside a makeshift mold

Confined by "what's normal" and "what's right"

Just do as you're told

Feeling quite old

washed up

strung out

No longer strong and bold

Please, take my hand to hold

So many regrets to live with

So much I took for granted

With a thousand moments I would give everything to relive

How does one treat life as a gift?

Do you open it slowly or open it swift?

If it's not what you wanted, do you fake happiness?

Or stay true to your soul and show that you're pissed?

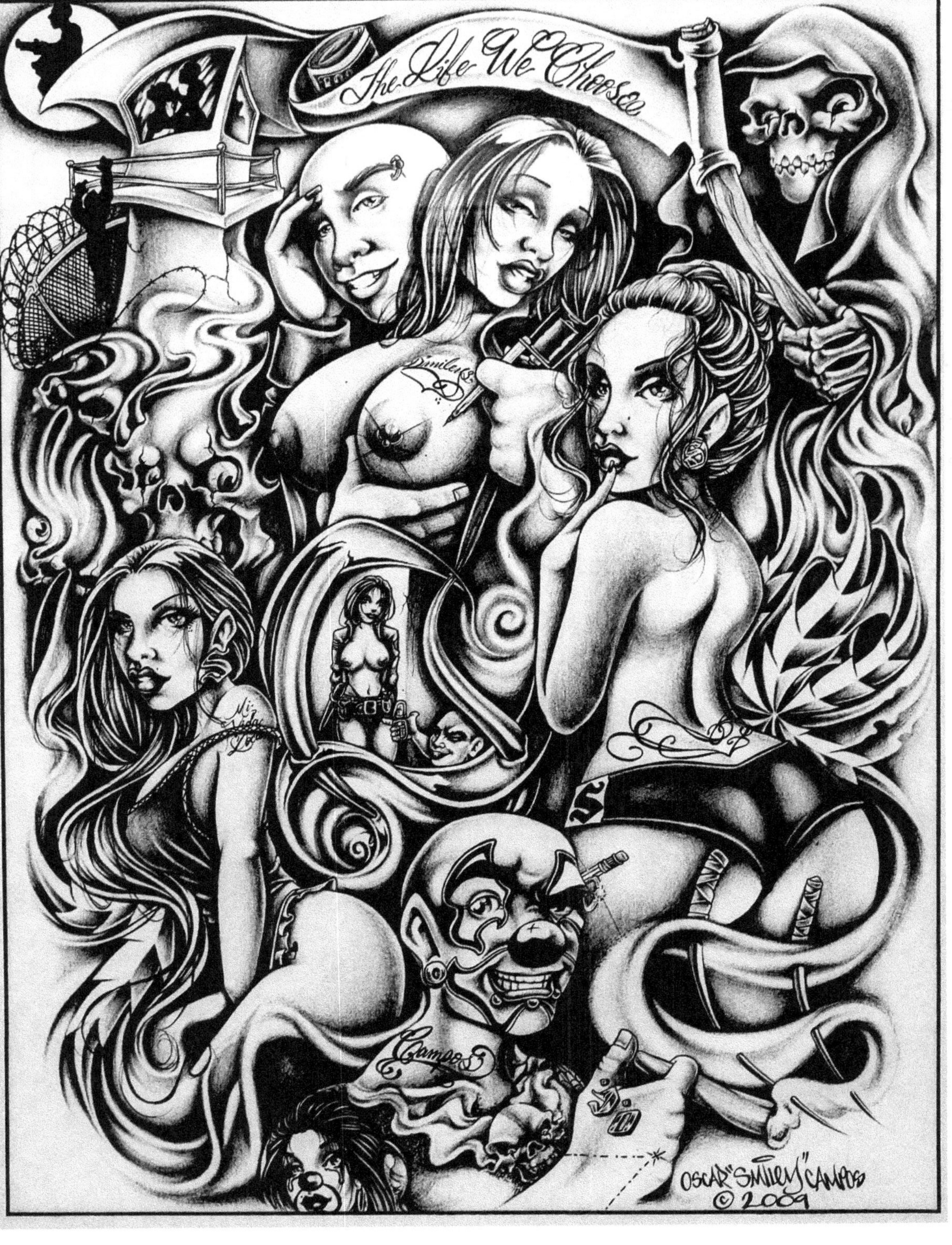
The Life We Choose
Oscar "Smiley" Campos
© 2009

CIRCUS LAMENT

Shoot it up
Cover up the ugly stuff
Wasted months, wasted years
following the beat of a busted drum
I need to be numb, ignorant, and dumb
Instead I stand, bitter and withered
"Come one, come all," I say, "Come hither!"
In love with a drug that's our number one killer
Take my wheel and steer
Can you touch my fears?
Tell me you're that special one, my sadness you can hear
That you will make it disappear
Looking at you is like looking in a mirror
Been up for days feeling weird

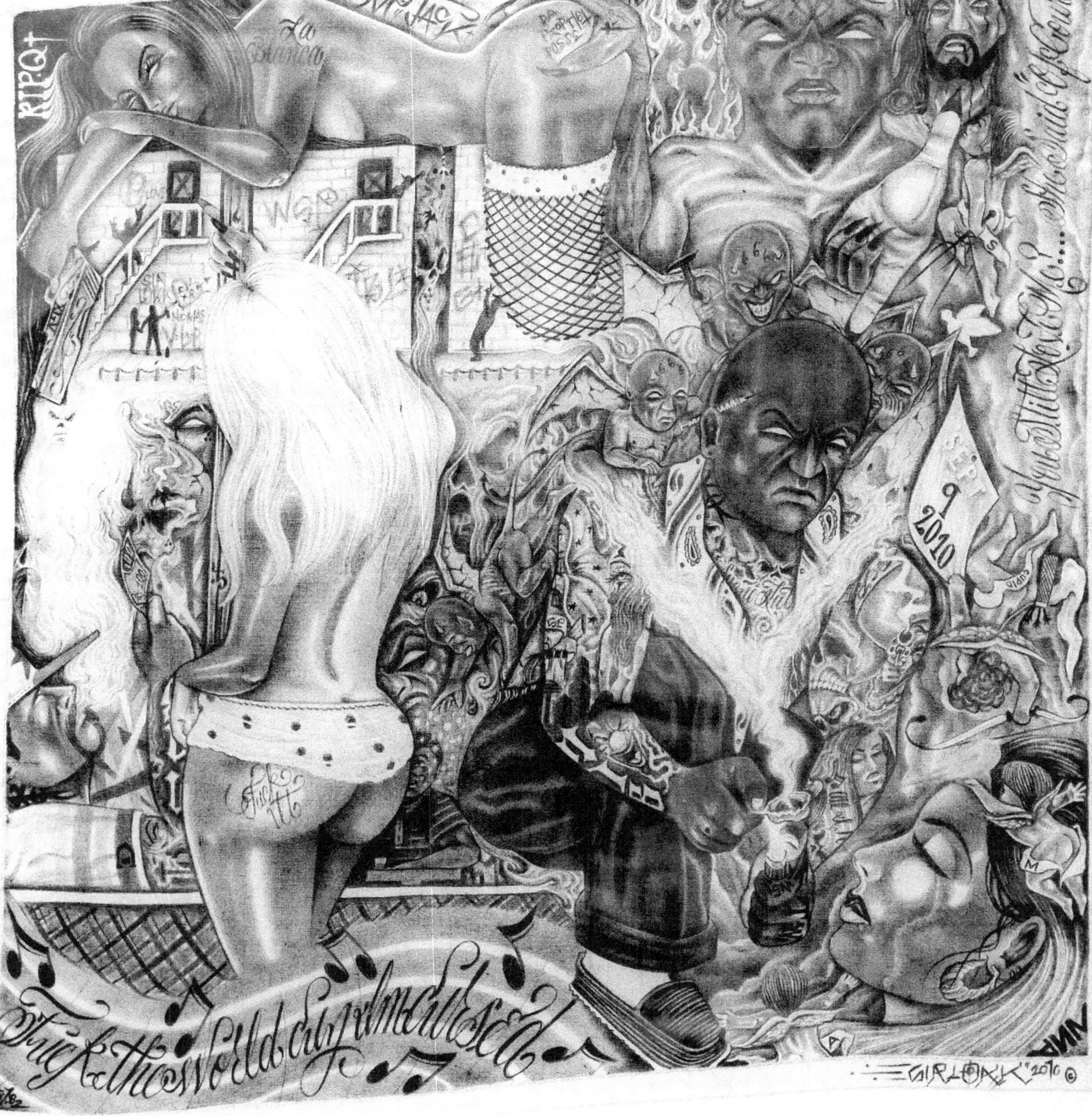

THE HUNT

Big fat sorry loser

Sickening pathetic lame-ass user

Giant motherfucking prick abuser

Live to die three times a day

Once when awakening

Once mid-way

and lastly before I close my eyes at night

But not before I prey

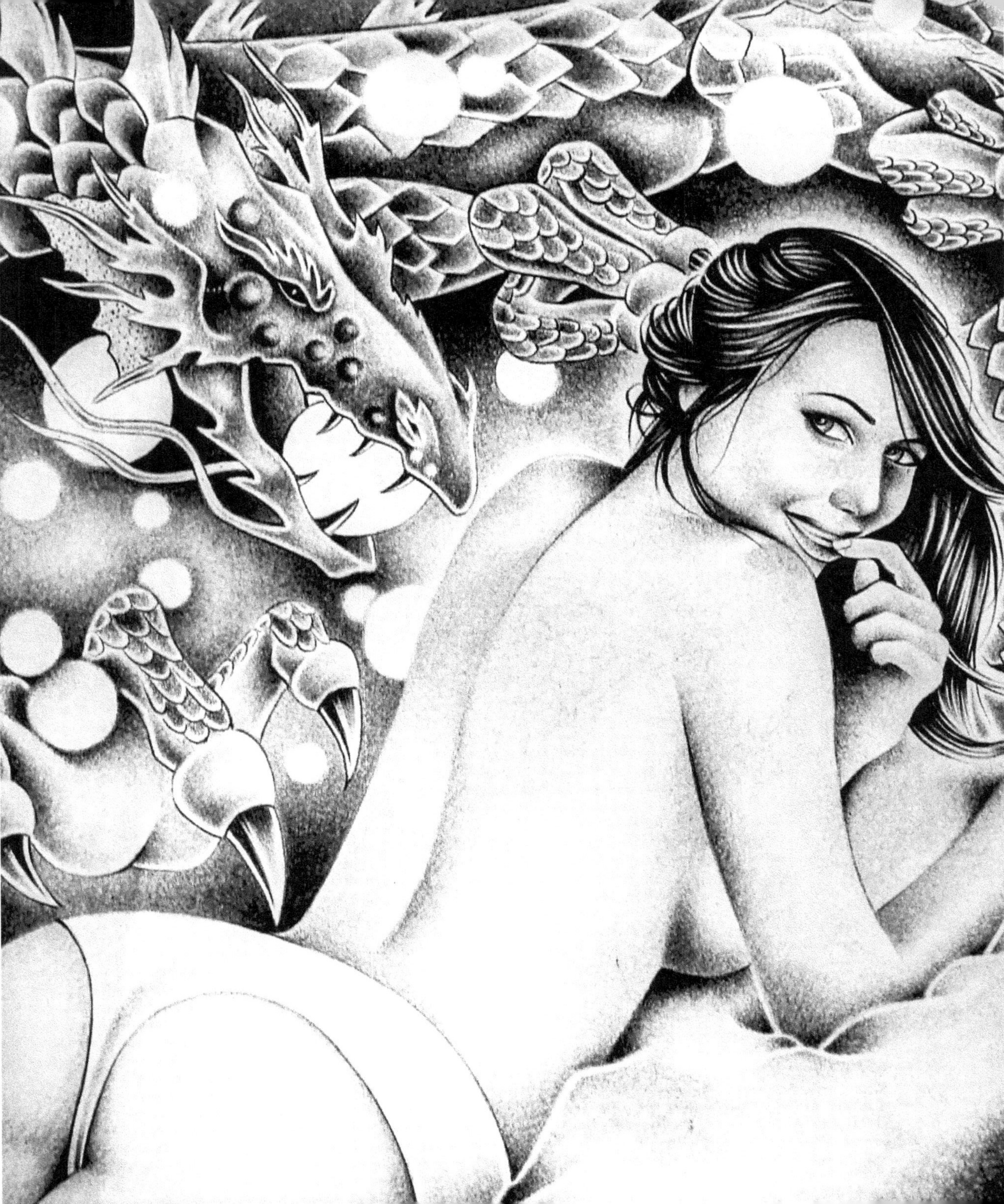

KENDRA'S POEM - RIP

Broken down, I walk the streets
These blisters hurt my hands and feet
Shuffling under starlit desert skies
again tonight tears blind my eyes
As I lay me down to sleep
this whole fucking story sounds so cheap
The Dunes Hotel, Van Buren Street
where Doc and I fled to escape the heat
My lover took a final flight
While I alone shivered that night
I'd hoped he never fly so high
Now my guardian angel is in the sky
"Yes, I know he had not tried"
"Yes, he and I had gotten high"
"Sir, I'm sorry your son died"
As I lay me down to sleep
still this story makes me weep
While cops all up and down the beat say:
"One more junkie off the street"

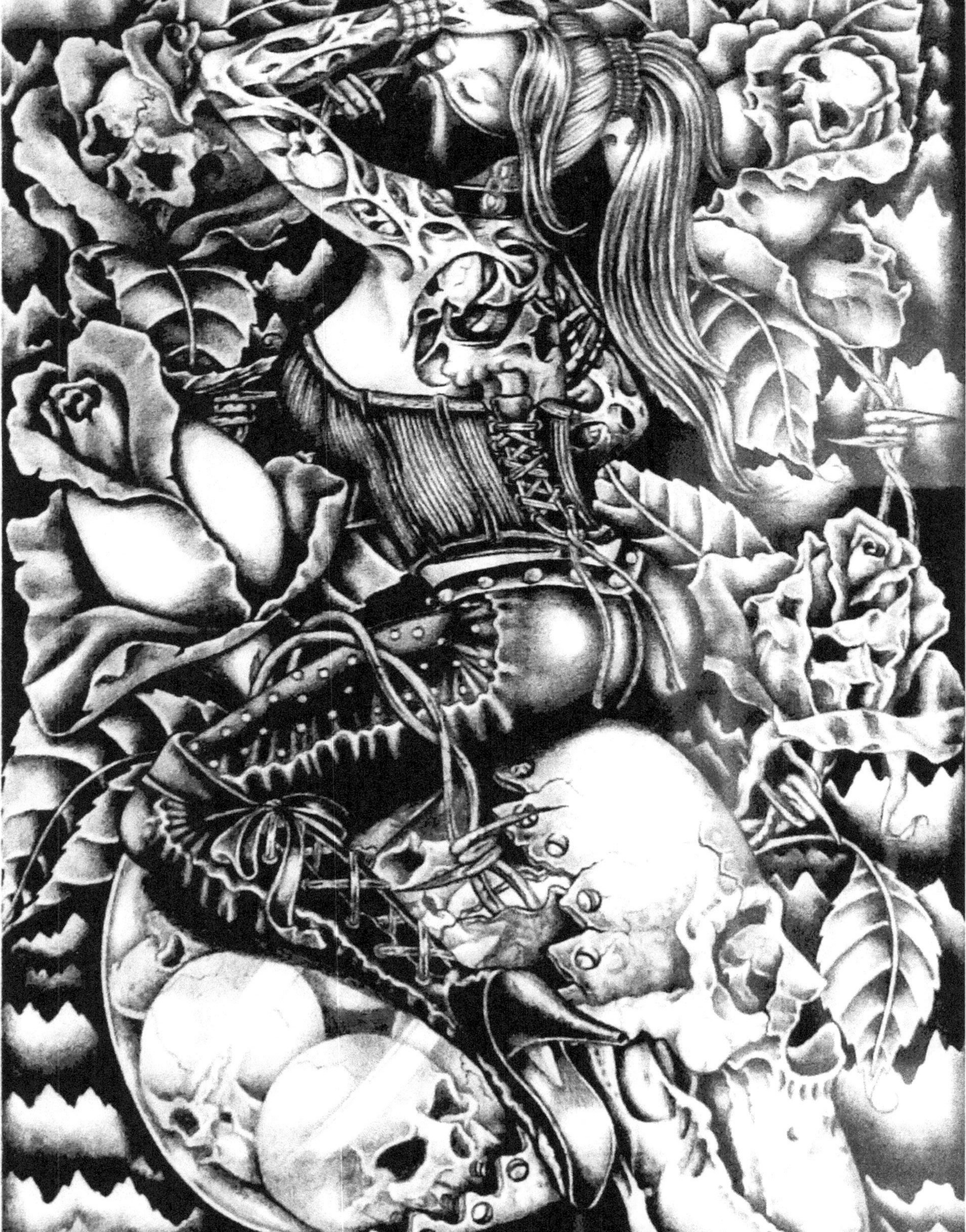

Going through the motions with exquisite ease

I'm starved of love and acceptance so I'm on my knees

For a quick fix-something to fill my endless need

This plank in my eye blurs my vision

making it impossible to see

Keeps me isolated to some degree

Still I decree

I shall do whatever I please!

But listen as I warn you: don't follow my lead

I sell out cheap

My addiction is a monstrous giant

Dangerous, jumpy, and full of greed

Desperate, lonely, unknowing, and phony

Still I bleed

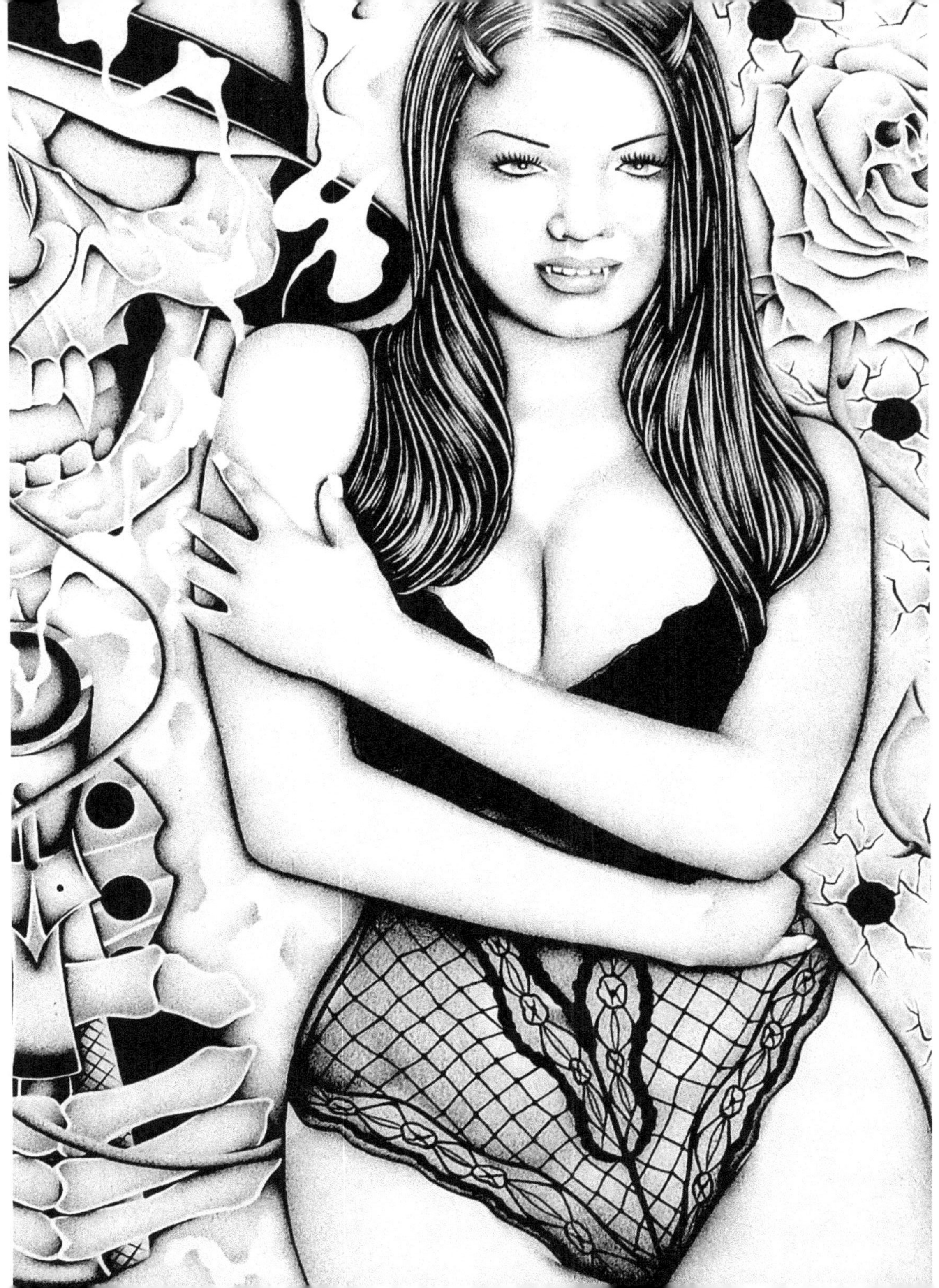

I am scared to be alone

I hate who I've become

I want a way out into complete oblivion

To be forever numb

The drugs stopped working long ago

Now I can't help but think about how to use a gun

Sobriety causes so much anxiety

I can't turn off my mind

It will never rest quietly

Life is too much to bear without a substance

Like being forced to watch a comet hurtling towards you

Destroying everything

as it plummets

Name anything

I've probably done it

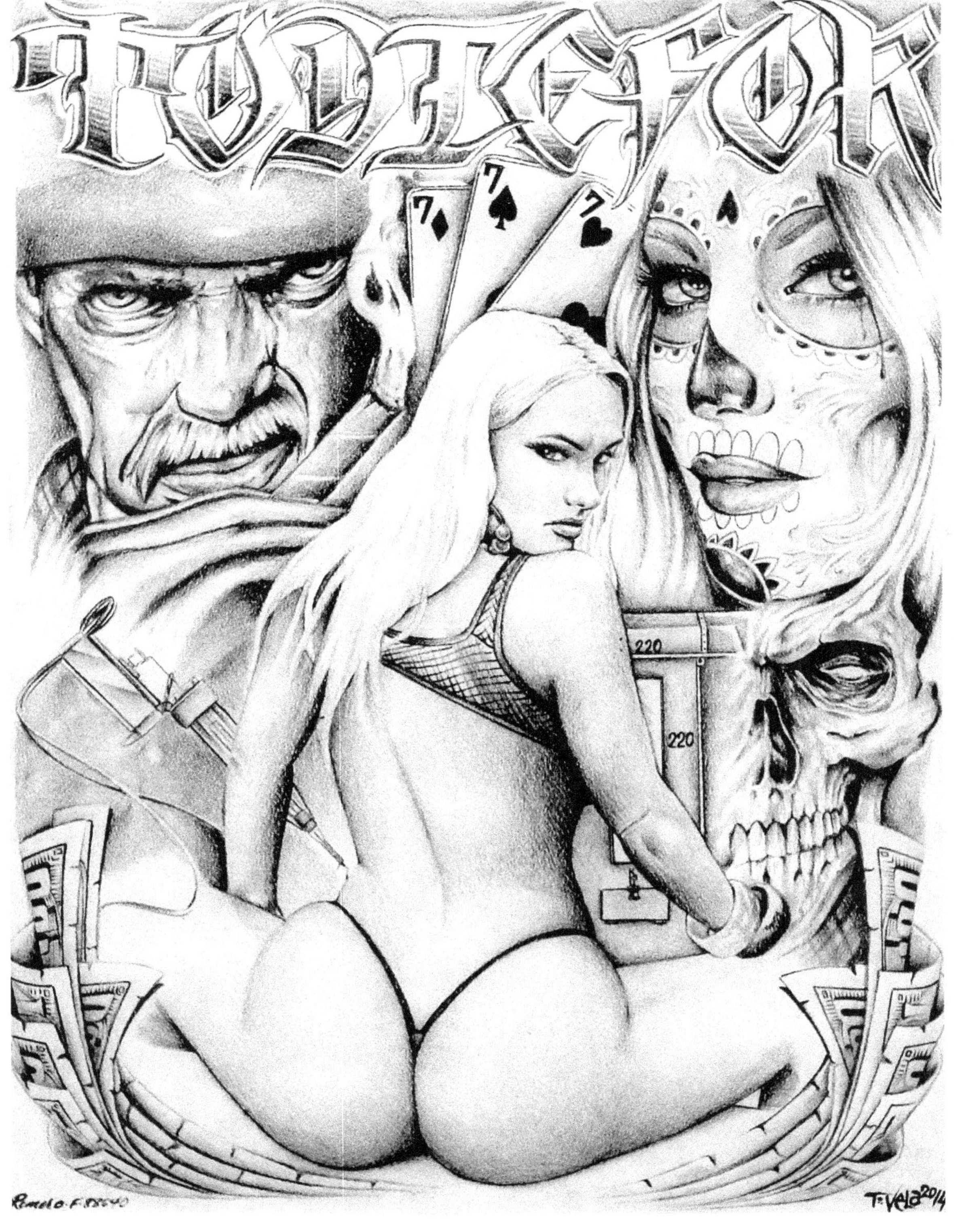
TODOKEYOK
T. Vela 2014

SHOWER THOUGHTS

Shower after shower yet the filth stays heavy on my skin
Scrubbing until I bleed because my pain is deep
as deep as my sins
I shy away from mirrors because my reflection's an infection
infusing me with fear
There is no reprieve from the bullshit because it's all in here
stinking up my soul
Not even a solid brick wall can keep it from getting near
Take a second look because not everyone is who they first appear
When I need a fix for loneliness
I just wave around cash
and to my side, dozens of friends will magically dash

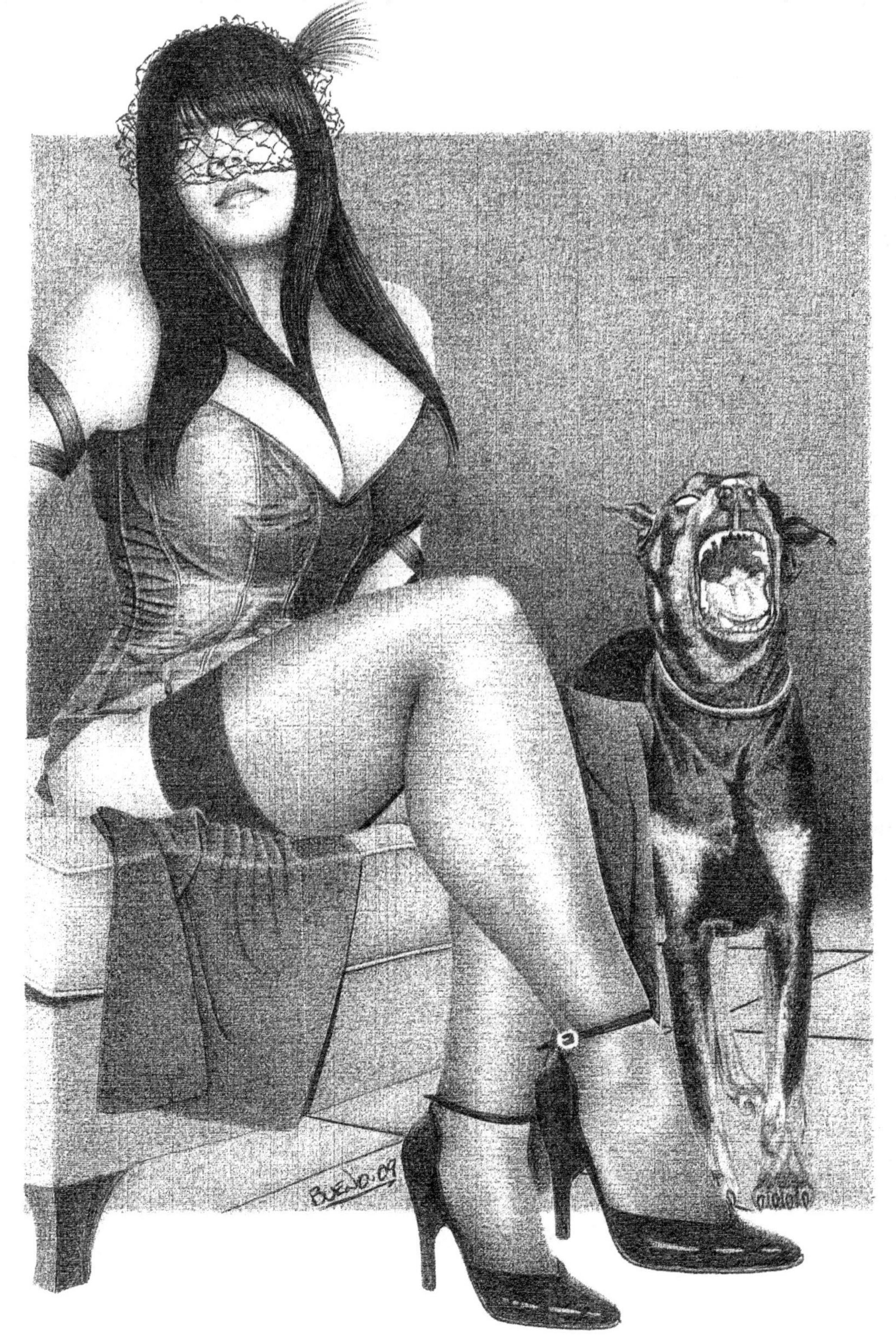

Unable, unwilling, refusing to grieve
A broken-down shell of my former self
Missing some needed piece
Hijacked
Overturned
Conquered by the beast
Suddenly I'm drowning
though just a moment ago
I was only knee deep

Wait!
I want a second chance!
Take me back to the cliff where I might have felt faith
Where I could have taken a leap
and maybe looked for the key
Now the water keeps rising
And no one to blame but me

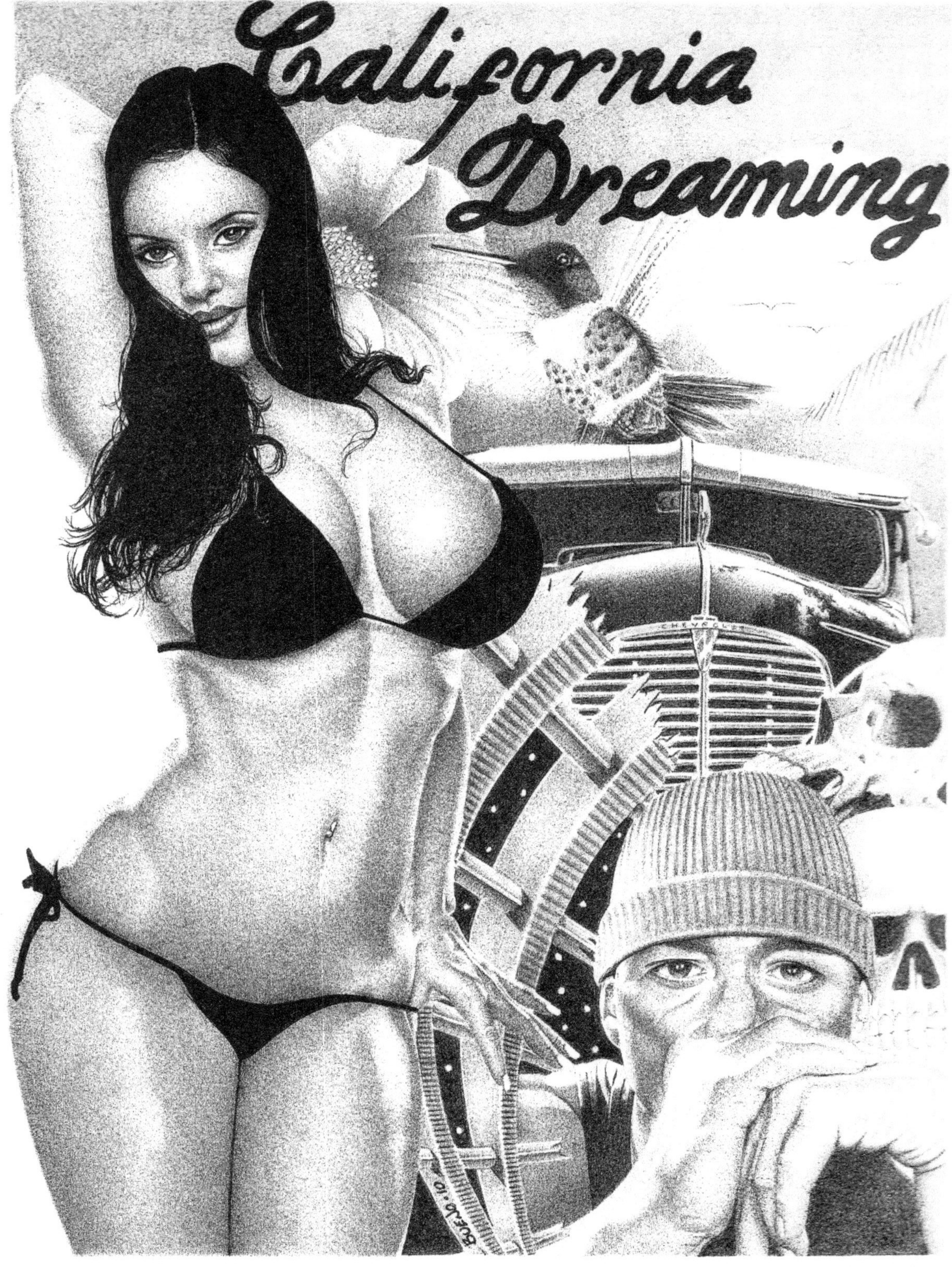

California
Dreaming

That's not who I am and I don't like to pretend
but the harder you push, the further I bend
I keep bending and bending and bending
but I just might break
if I'm pushed again
Each hurt I grind into small pieces
for the monster inside me
He has layed low
and really was mostly sleeping
But the more you hurt me
the more I keep feeding
Now he is gigantic and started multiplying and breeding
His claws gash my insides causing significant bleeding
My body temperature is rising from this hot-tempered breathing
The monster is unmanageable
and I can't stop him from unleashing

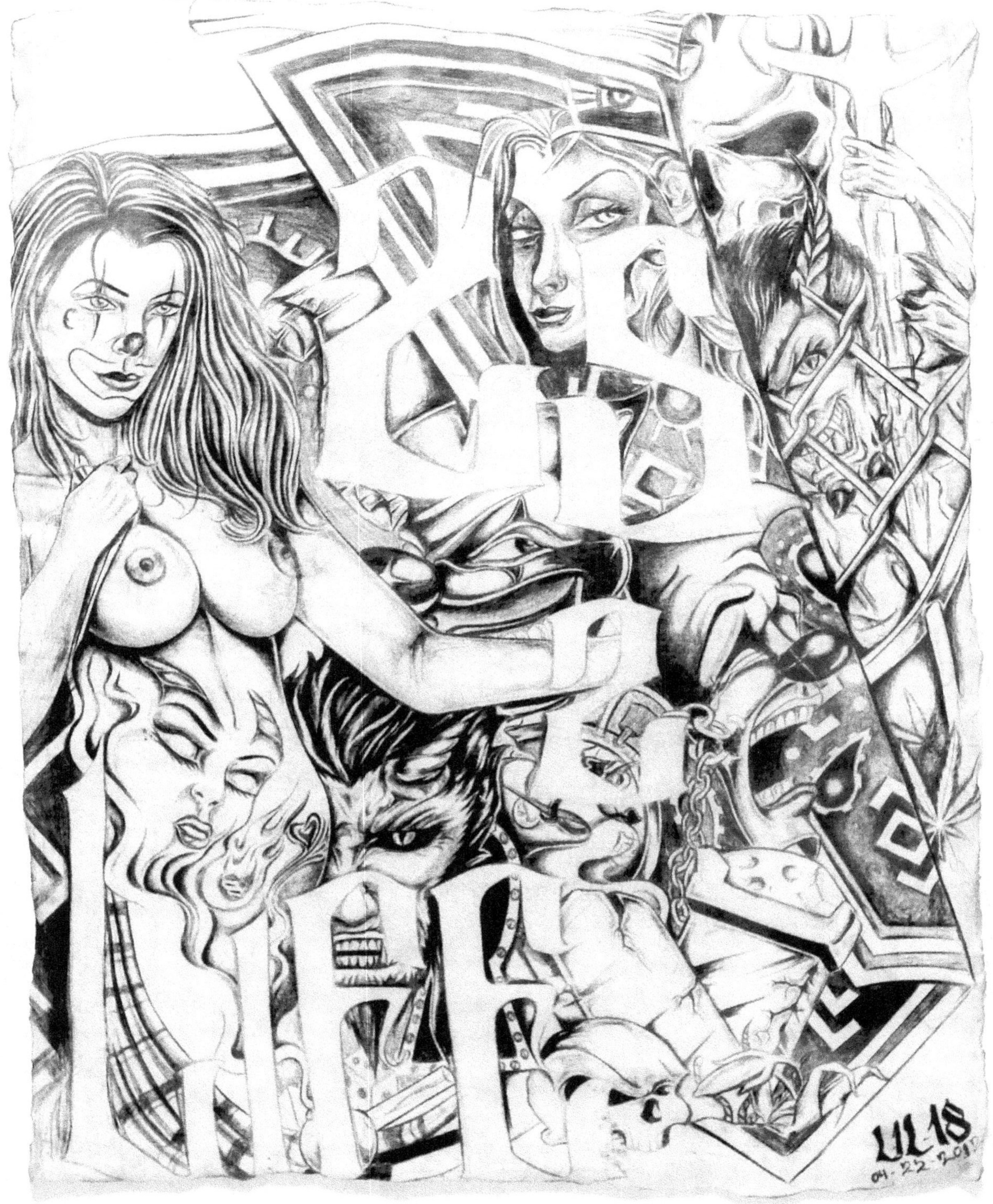
UL 18
04-22-20__

And here I stand, having been pushed and pulled
I twist and I bend
Blowing away in the wind
I'm lost and alone in my sea of excuses
A story told through cuts, scars, fresh wounds, and ugly bruises

Go ahead and take advantage of my kindness
It's the part of my being that everyone uses
Zero wins and one thousand five hundred and thirty-eight loses

Look at me
So pathetic and lame
Oh, you can't look at my face?
That's because I'm covered with filth and camouflaged by shame
So many hours spent scrubbing and cleaning
yet still,
I look the same

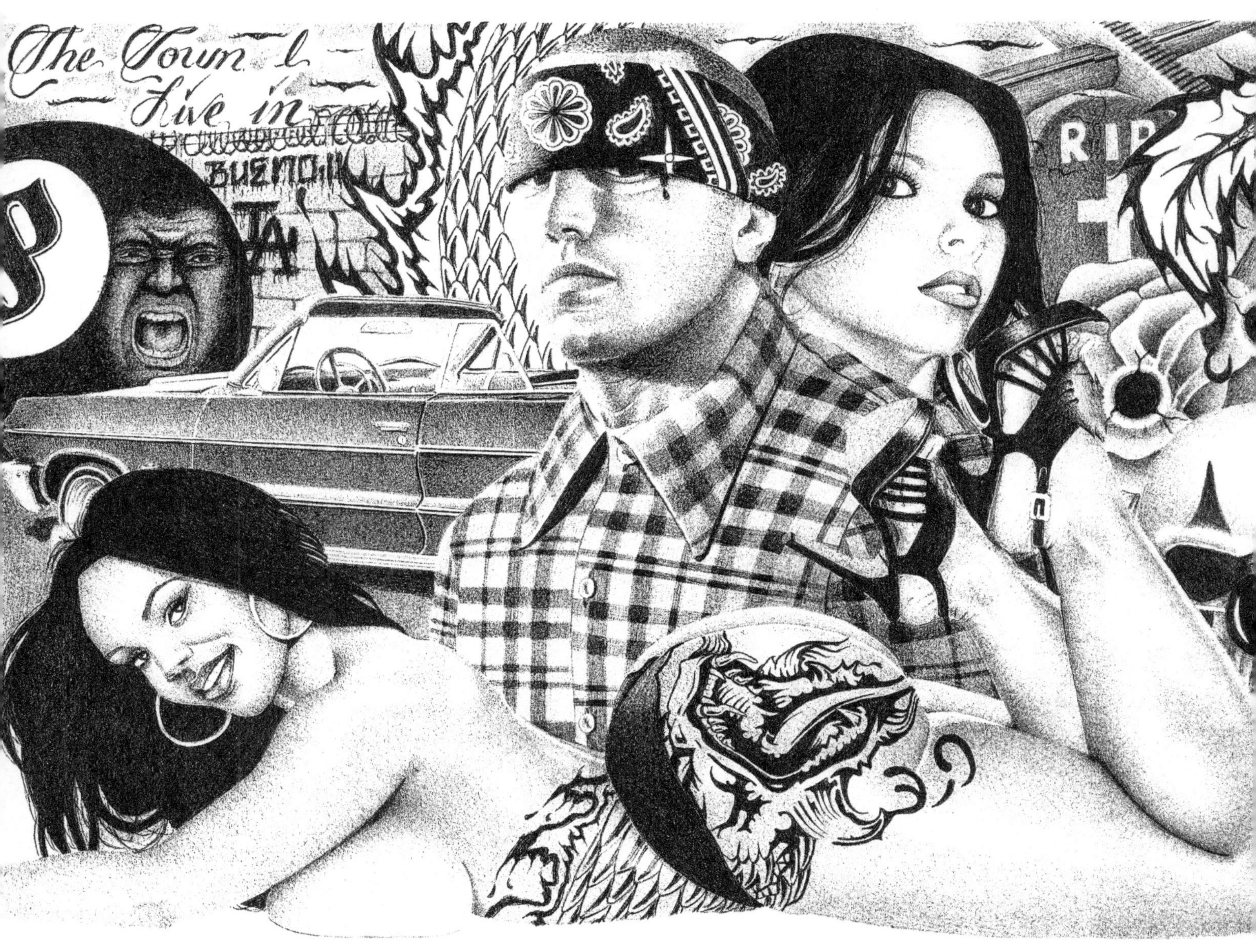
The Town I
Live in
BUENO
RIP

Everything I get or have is mine and only mine
Because I'm a real motherfucker
You know, one of a kind
Not quite broker than the lies you tell
Think you got me fooled
But I know your lines and schemes all too well
The only person you're fooling is yourself
I can walk away and be fine at any time
Escaping from this mother-child caregiver-caretaker living hell
I emphasize the importance of building a life and making a name
But you're comfortable doing nothing
So nothing is what you'll gain

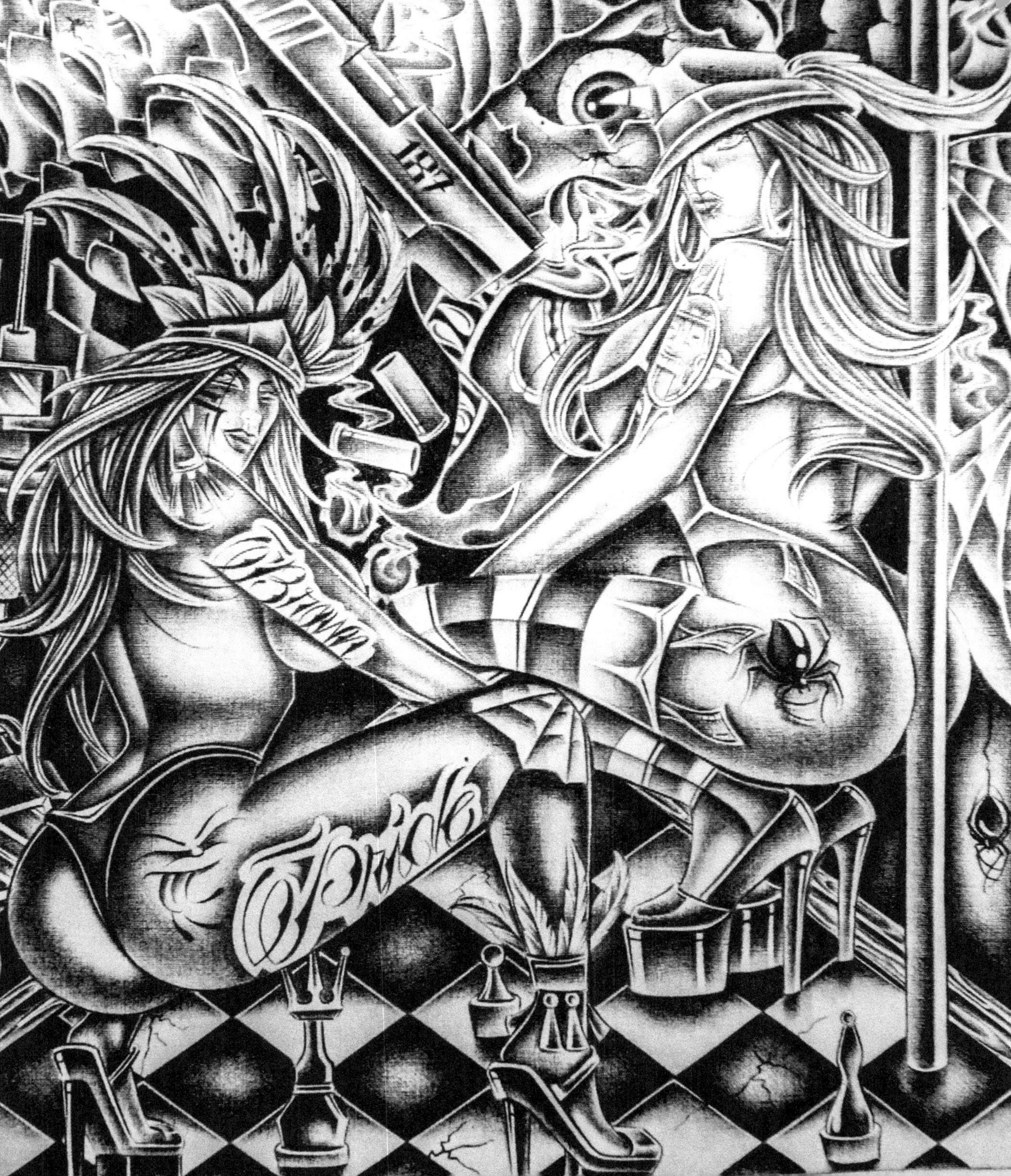
Brown
Pride

AGREE TO DISAGREE

Agree to close my eyes so you can do as you please
We bled together during battle until I discovered
we were fighting for different teams
I crucify myself every day, every night
I will crucify myself until I finally get it right
As much as I hate me,
I'm quite thankful I'm not you
I'd saw off each foot before I'd take a step in those shoes
Refuse all hands and never take advantage
Smile sweetly and look everyone in the eyes
Especially when telling lies
In life's pageant, leave nothing behind,
Pick up every piece and every fragment
so when there's an opportunity to escape
I can leave without causing any real permanent damage
But before I slide away, please take this gift
of all the guilt I felt
but it was really meant for you
You're big and you're tough
I'm sure you can handle it

AFTERTHOUGHT

I lie back
Close my eyes
Contemplate the Bridge of Sighs
I didn't make a change in what she was going through
Sometimes, I think I never wanted to
With a fist full of twenties I can arrange
some poppy-sap refreshment to ease her pain

You can bet I'm feeling free
'cuz chains like hers
ain't the chains holdin' me

Money talks
Bullshit walks
It's what I know and all I see
If you're in doubt, then start to shout
Your heart has the lock and heroin is the key
So do as I say
or go away
You have a need, a hungry arm to feed,
and you'll be back another day

I know quite well the price you pay
in leaving hell for a short reprieve
For it takes all and you can't leave
Stuck in an endless circle since your fall
Listen close and you'll hear the call

Rest here, my dear, and have no fears
Put out your arm and dry those tears
For a little while, I'll make you smile
Leave your panties in that dirty pile
and close your eyes as I lick your thighs
You knew I wasn't sellin' any alibis,
and it's much too late to hear you cry
You once had a life
But now you die

Rachel Wrong continues to explore her emotions and experiences through poetry and art.

Today she is living in the Pacific Northwest.

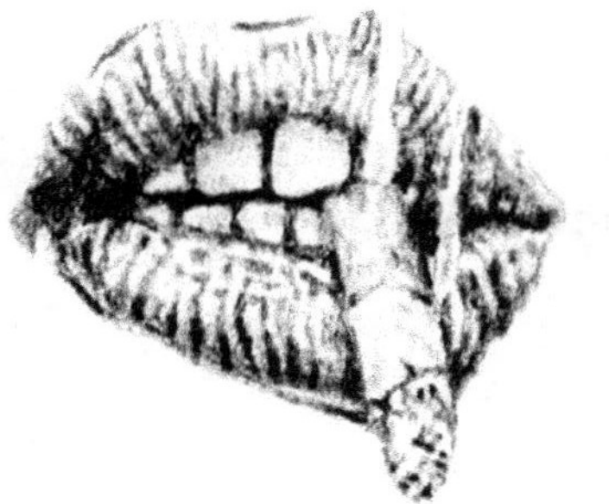

Poems selected and edited by Lily J. Noonan and Gregg Stone
Prison art from the Stone Collection

Original cover art created by Gregg Stone
Poem typeface in JohnDoe; additional text in Adobe Garamond Pro

ISBN 978-1946341082

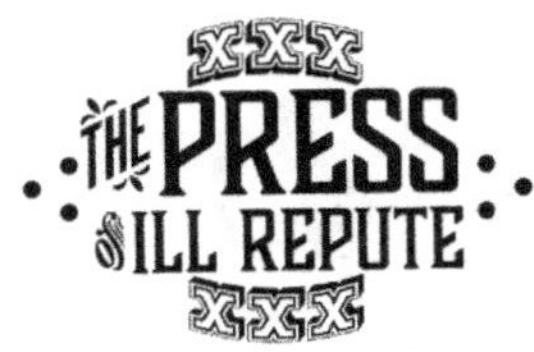

First Edition

OTHER TITLES FEATURING RACHEL WRONG

COLLAGE DE RACHEL WRONG

featuring photos by Lily J. Noonan; illustrations by Gregg Stone

HOMEFREE

scheduled for late 2024 release

MORE TITLES FROM THE PRESS OF ILL REPUTE

SEX AND LUST IN TIJUANA: TRUE SEX STORIES OF THE TJ AMIGOS

THE WANDERER IN TIJUANA: GAMBLING, LIQUOR, PONIES, GIRLS, HIGH LIFE, 'N EVERYTHING